BOULTBEES WOOD

MEIGHS WOOD

Marlbrook

CHURCH WOOD

CHANTRY WOOD

MERIDEN SHAFTS WOOD

WALSH HALL

Meriden open fields?

MERIDEN HALL POOLS

Moat House

MERIDEN HALL

ALSPATH

MILLISONS WOOD

CROW WOOD

MARSTON HALL

BICKENHILL HEATH   PARK FARM

HILL BICKENHILL

Holywell Brook

MIDDLE BICKENHILL

STONEBRIDGE

Coventre way

CHURCH BICKENHILL

HARGRAVE

DIDDINGTON

R. Blythe

DUNSTAL HEATH

Shadow Brook

MERIDEN HEATH

Castle Hills

Hampton Brook

BLACK ALDER MEADOW

HAR HALL

HAMPTON DEMESNE

INNAGE

MILL POOL

HAMPTON COPPICE

Gorsey Lane   Park Lane

MEADOW OF HAMPTON

Low Brook

Horn Brook

Giants Den

BARBERS COPPICE

HAMPTON in ARDEN

Moat House

Salters Lane

ASBURIES COPPICE

BROWNS MEADOW

Back Lane

CATHERINE DE BARNES HEATH

Walford Hall

MERCOTE

Berry Hall

PACKHORSE BRIDGE

Mercote Hall

MERCOTE

The Moat

HENWOOD MILL

BROAD MEADOW

RYTON END

BERKSWELL PARK

BERKSWELL

HAWKHURST MOOR

RAVENSHAW

CALDECOFORDE MILL

EASTCOTE   THORNTON MEADOW

BRADNOCKS MARSH STEW

HENWOOD HEATH

Eastcote Hall

BENTON GREEN

Miry Lane

HENWOOD PRIORY

Grimshaws Moat

BRADNOCKS MILL

RUFFE CLOSE

Ram Hall

COPT HEATH

BARSTON

LAVENDER HALL

Moat House

Purnell Brook

BARSTON PARK

BARSTON MARSH

OLDHALL END   CAROL GREEN

Reeves Green

ongdon Hall

PIERCIL END

Inn

BALSALL STREET

NEEDLERS END

Barriesplace

NAILCOTE

KNOWLE   Kixley Lane

PARK FIELDS

BEECH WOOD

BEANIT WOOD

KNOWLE HALL

TEMPLE BALSALL

LAND OF THE KNIGHTS TEMPLAR

KNOWLE DEMESNE ?

BERKSWELL COMMON

POOL WOOD

HEATH

Moat Close

Cuttle Brook

CUTTLE MILL

KNOWLE WOOD

ROTTON ROW

CUTTLE POOL

BURTON GREEN

KNOWLE GROVE

CHADWICK

BALSALL COMMON

BLUE LAKE HOUSE

NORTON GREEN

Rudfyn Lane

RRIDGE WOOD

Oldwich

Fen End Farm

To Kenilworth

DARLEY MILL

DARLEY GREEN

Netherwood

NETHERWOOD HEATH

1990

Peter Lewellyn

Mayor. Solihull M.B.C.

June 1993.

THE BOOK OF GREATER SOLIHULL

FRONT COVER: Solihull High Street c1910. (DG)

Solihull, new and old 1983. (SL)

THE BOOK OF GREATER SOLIHULL

BY

JOY WOODALL

BARRACUDA BOOKS LIMITED
BUCKINGHAM, ENGLAND
MCMXC

PUBLISHED BY BARRACUDA BOOKS LIMITED
BUCKINGHAM, ENGLAND
AND PRINTED BY
NUFFIELD PRESS LIMITED
OXFORD, ENGLAND

BOUND BY
DOTESIOS PRINTERS LIMITED
TROWBRIDGE, ENGLAND

LITHOGRAPHY BY
FORE COLOUR GRAPHICS
HERTFORD, ENGLAND

JACKETS PRINTED BY
CHENEY & SONS LIMITED
BANBURY, OXON

TYPESET BY
PHOENIX MANOR
MILTON KEYNES, ENGLAND

© Joy Woodall 1990

ISBN 0 86023 443 6

Contents

The chapter headings are taken from Edge-Hill, *a poem in four books by Richard Jago (1715-81).*

Acknowledgements

Without the kindness and generosity of many people, researching and writing this book, which covers such a large area, would have been difficult. For sharing their local and specialist knowledge and making material available to me I should like to thank Connie, Dee and Jean, Mrs D. Agutter, Wendy Burnett, Bob Farmer, Dr Margaret Gelling, Dr Denis Gray, Neil Lang, Graham Smith and the late Robert Shaw. My greatest debt, however, is to the late Leighton Bishop who, with the late Mollie Varley, researched deeply into the history of much of the area in the 1970s. As a beneficiary of their material my task has been greatly lightened.

Thanks are also due to the staff at Warwick Record Office, at the Shakespeare Birthplace Record Office, in the Department of Archaeology at Birmingham Museum for their assistance, and particularly to the staff at Solihull Library for their unfailing support. The latter have also held the subscription lists which made publication of this book possible.

I am grateful to those who have lent photographs, to Councillor Richard Lewis who initially suggested the book, to the Mayor, Councillor Ken Meeson, for agreeing to write the Foreword, and last but not least to Sue Bates. She has continually encouraged and advised me, made valuable criticisms of the text and given freely of her time.

On a more practical note I would like to thank Bob for his maps, and my new typist for his patience. He has battled manfully with my handwriting and the word processor, the manual in one hand and the dictionary in the other.

Key to Caption Credits

Reproduced by kind permission of:

LB	the late Leighton Bishop	IS	the family of the late Mrs I. Silver
AC	Mrs A. Curtis	SL	Solihull Library
DG	Dr Denis Gray	KJS	Mrs K.J. Startin
TG	T. Guest	ROS	the family of the late R.O. Suffield
MF	the Markham Family	WF	the Warmingham Family
JM	J. Marks	WCRO	Warwickshire County Record Office
RS	the late R. Shaw	AW	Mrs A. Wood
	JW	J. Woodall	

Modern maps drawn by Bob Park.

Foreword

by Cllr Ken Meeson, Mayor of Solihull

The Borough of Solihull, set in the very heart of England, has a history and a style which evokes fond memories for many residents but of which newcomers and visitors know little.

My wife, Annette, spent a happy childhood in one of the cottages in Mill Lane so it gives me a special pleasure to write this short foreword and to thank Joy Woodall for producing such a well-researched and detailed history of the Borough.

Sadly, like so much of old Solihull, the cottages in Mill Lane were swept away in the 1960s' frenzy of 'improvements and redevelopment' and to many the pace of change continues to threaten the character and identity of our area. There is still, however, something special about Solihull, with its diversity from ancient Smiths Wood and Castle Bromwich in the north to the grandeur of St Alphege and Malvern Hall in the south; from the quietness of Berkswell to the modern bustle of the International Airport; from Edwardian elegance at Olton to the modern development of Monkspath.

Pressures here as elsewhere continue with the demands for new housing, new industries and the massive increase in traffic as motorways converge on the Borough, but it remains a pleasant place to live and work as we strive to maintain the integrity of our motto *Urbs in Rure* (Town in the Country) for future generations. I hope that this book will help to remind us of our rich heritage and encourage the people of the Borough to cherish and preserve the unique character of Solihull.

Dedication

For Leighton

9

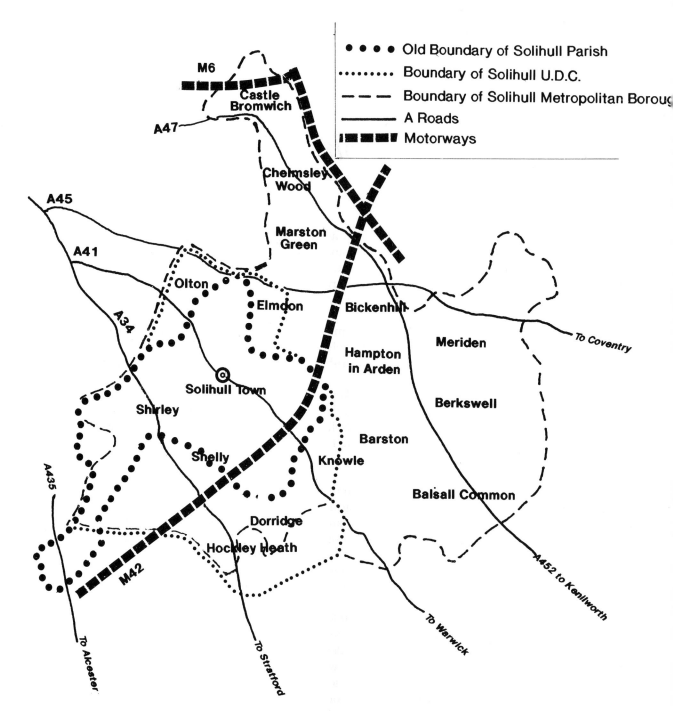

Map of Solihull Boundaries — ancient and modern.

Hail Solihull!

The name Solihull means 'miry or muddy hill', an apt description of the hill beside St Alphege Church as it was in the past, especially in damp weather. Then the natural surface of the stiff red marl turned to sticky mud, which adhered to the feet, impressed the memory and created a place-name. Since Solihull acquired its name, many centuries ago, Church Hill has been greatly worn away and is now less steep and memorable while Solihull has become a town, a parish, and a Metropolitan Borough.

The town of Solihull, as we see it today, is very much the result of post-1960 re-development. It is neat, attractive, thriving, with purpose-built public buildings, a pleasant shopping centre and quality office accommodation. Yet the mediaeval parish church and scatter of old buildings indicate that the town's past is long.

Founded some 800 years ago, especially as a market centre, Solihull was a mediaeval 'new town'. For about two hundred years it traded successfully, then gradually its market fell into decline. By the mid-17th century it had virtually ceased and Solihull became a small country town lying at the heart of an extensive rural parish. Throughout the 18th and most of the 19th centuries agriculture was the chief occupation, Solihull remaining wholly rural, only 3,401 people occupying its 11,000 acres in 1841.

The opening in 1852 of Solihull railway station, on the Great Western Railway line to Paddington, brought the town within commuting distance of Birmingham. At first, however, a mere trickle of people moved out to take advantage of the clean air and healthy atmosphere of Solihull. The initial newcomers were prosperous manufacturers who took the larger houses in the High Street and the grander farmhouses close to the town. From the 1860s facilities improved: gas, street lighting, pavements and sewerage were installed. To serve new residents more shops opened and a wider and more sophisticated range of goods and services became available. In subsequent years a fair amount of building took place and a few new roads were cut, but it was 1891 before the population reached 5,000, and 1911 before it passed the 10,000 mark.

Nationally in the late Victorian period, a new system of local government was created, District Councils replacing the old parish administration. Under the Local Government Act of 1894 Solihull became a Rural District Council (RDC) concerned with the affairs of 10 other country parishes: Baddesley Clinton, Barston, Balsall, Bushwood, Elmdon, Knowle, Lapworth, Nuthurst, Packwood, Tanworth-in-Arden, as well as those of Solihull: a total of 41,807 acres. Each village sent one or more elected representatives, the Council consisting of 18 members. Initially it was difficult to find people who had the time and the will to stand for election and the first councillors were local squires, clergymen and wealthy landowners; unusually for the period there was one woman councillor, Elizabeth Ramsden, who represented Knowle. The meetings were held in the boardroom of Solihull Workhouse, a small professional staff of Surveyor, Treasurer, Inspector of Nuisance, part-time Clerk and shared Medical Officer carrying out the Council's decisions. These were mostly concerned with public health and public works: sewerage, street lighting, highways and the fire brigade. There was no 'council office' at first; the Surveyor worked from his house in The Square and later from a rented room. The Clerk was similarly accommodated.

About 1905 a permanent Council Office was established in Streetsbrook Road. On the site now occupied by the Fire Station a Council Depôt was set up and two cottages built, one to house the Surveyor and the other the Clerk to the Council. From here and rented rooms around the town, the area was administered until the mid-1930s.

In the 50 years 1881 to 1931 Solihull grew steadily but slowly. New houses, the majority good-sized detached family homes or large semi-detached villas, often in groups, were built along the chief routes into the town and several new roads — Herbert, Homer, Ashleigh, Alderbrook, The Crescent, Silhill Hall, Broad Oaks, Brueton Avenue — cut at the perimeter. New roads and houses were also built in three other parts of the District, at Dorridge: Knowle Wood, Dorridge, Station and Temple Roads; at Olton: St Bernard's, Kineton Green, Westbourne and Reservoir Roads; and at Shirley in Blossomfield, Solihull and Stratford Roads. There were, however, still many farms, winding lanes, deep hedgerows and large areas of unspoilt countryside between the villages and around the new roads. But Solihull was set for change: under the provisions of the Warwickshire Review Order of 1932 the RDC was swept away, the wholly rural parishes of Bushwood, Lapworth, Baddesley Clinton, Barston and Balsall, and part of Tanworth-in-Arden were transferred to other councils. Solihull became an Urban District, the 21 members of the new Council administering a smaller Solihull: 20,365 acres with a population of 25,373.

The growth of Solihull after 1932 was phenomenal. Shirley, already the largest of the settlements, grew particularly rapidly as large housing estates (such as the Shakespeare Manor Estate) covered the fields. New schools, including Sharmans Cross Senior, were built and one or two small factories erected. In seven years the population of the Urban District doubled, then the outbreak of war brought building to a stop. Instead of houses, and much against the Council's wishes, two large factories were built as part of the Government's 'shadow factory' scheme — one off Lode Lane by Rover Cars and the other in Marshall Lake Road by British Small Arms (BSA) — all production being geared to the war effort.

After the war the shadow factories were permitted to remain and Rover, having purchased a further 200 acres of land, decided to make Solihull its headquarters. The small factories at Cranmore expanded into a trading estate and a second estate was begun beside Lode Lane. As soon as building restrictions were lifted new houses, both private and council, started to go up again.

Sir Patrick Abercrombie, in his plan for the West Midlands, had designated Solihull suitable for growth with an optimum population of 112,000. Such a large number of people would require more than just homes, and plans for new schools, roads, shops, and recreational facilities were formulated. New administrative buildings would also be needed, for the Council Offices, situated in the old Public Hall, Poplar Road (rebuilt and renamed the Council House since 1937) were already too small to house all departments. A civic centre, including offices, a large lecture hall and library, were therefore envisaged for the new Solihull.

In 1954 the Queen gave her consent to Solihull being granted a Charter of Incorporation as a Municipal Borough. Princess Margaret visited the town and, at a ceremony at the Odeon Cinema, Shirley presented the charter scroll to the Mayor Designate, the town's first Mayor for some 300 years. Large crowds thronged the be-flagged streets, there was a civic lunch and the Princess appeared on the Council House balcony.

In the 1950s a few properties within the town were demolished to make way for new buildings but the populace in general appeared not to be aware of the magnitude of the changes soon to occur. From 1961-7 the central area was under re-development, the buildings in Mill Lane, Drury Lane, part of the High Street and Warwick Road, some of them mediaeval, being replaced by the Mell Square shopping centre.

During these years work on the new civic area was begun, the Queen opening the Civic Hall (now the Conference and Banqueting Centre) in 1962. The Council Offices and Civic Suite were in use by 1968 and the fine new library with integral theatre completed by 1976. All these buildings became increasingly necessary, for by then Solihull had grown larger than even Abercrombie had estimated.

The population of Solihull by 1961 was 96,000 but, as a Borough, it was subservient to Warwickshire County Council, which controlled all major services and took two thirds of the income from the rates. Consequently Solihull, in search of greater independence, applied for and was granted County Borough status from April 1964. Ten short years later, under the Local Government re-organisation of 1974, Solihull was created a Metropolitan District, one of seven within the newly formed West Midlands county. The Borough immediately doubled in size as the civil parishes of Balsall, Barston, Berkswell, Castle Bromwich, Chelmsley Wood, Fordbridge, Hampton-in-Arden, Hockley Heath, Kingshurst and Meriden were taken in: a total of 44,495 acres with a population of about 200,000. The northern and western parts of the Metropolitan Borough are almost totally urban, Chelmsley Wood, Kingshurst and Fordbridge having been transformed from rural tranquillity by Birmingham overspill. The parishes in the east of the Borough are still chiefly rural and there are many working farms.

All these settlements, urban and rural, have a past, a history of their own, which is now part of the total history of the Metropolitan Borough of Solihull. Hopefully this will, in some measure, be revealed in *The Book of Greater Solihull.*

Church Hill 1909; the miry hill which gave Solihull its name. (SL)

ABOVE: The Square, Solihull c1820. On the left Linden House, the George Inn and Park House. To the right of the Church may be seen the edge of the Town Hall and the stocks. (WCRO) BELOW: Streetsbrook Road c1900. The building stands approximately where Miall Park Road is now. (SL)

14

ABOVE: Outside Shirley Church, Stratford Road, looking towards Birmingham c1900. (SL) BELOW: The bottom of Church Hill c1910 with the entrance to Homer Road on the right. The two men stand beside a gate giving access to a field path. (DG)

ABOVE: Ravenswood, Homer Road, typical of the houses built in Solihull 1880-1930. Demolished 1983. (SL) BELOW: Solihull from the church tower c1910. (SL)

16

ABOVE: Shopping in the High Street c1930. (WCRO) BELOW: The old
Council House, Poplar Road, decorated for Princess Margaret's visit in 1954.
Built in 1876 as the Public Hall, it was the centre of Solihull social life. (SL)

ABOVE: Princess Margaret discusses the Borough mace with Councillor R. Cooper, the Mayor Designate, on Charter Day 1954. (SL) BELOW: The Fire Station, Streetsbrook Road, previously the Council Depôt, c1960. The houses, right, are those built c1905 for the Surveyor and Clerk to the Council. (SL)

18

ABOVE: Adverts for the type of small firms taking premises on the new Trading Estates in the 1950s. The Boardman factory was the first on the Lode Lane Estate in 1953. Econa was started by W.E. Wright, who was the Mayor in 1957. BELOW: The final Council meeting in the old Chamber, Poplar Road, January 1968. (SL)

ABOVE: Mill Lane and Drury Lane c1960, prior to their demolition and redevelopment. (SL) BELOW: The Civic Hall, new Council offices and Civic Suite, opened in stages 1962-8. (SL)

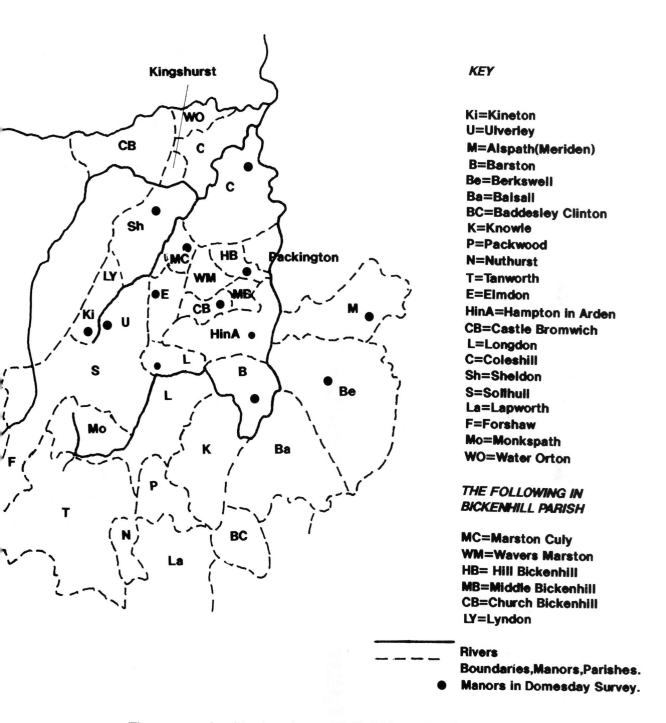

Ki=Kineton
U=Ulverley
M=Alspath(Meriden)
B=Barston
Be=Berkswell
Ba=Balsall
BC=Baddesley Clinton
K=Knowle
P=Packwood
N=Nuthurst
T=Tanworth
E=Elmdon
HinA=Hampton in Arden
CB=Castle Bromwich
L=Longdon
C=Coleshill
Sh=Sheldon
S=Solihull
La=Lapworth
F=Forshaw
Mo=Monkspath
WO=Water Orton

**THE FOLLOWING IN
BICKENHILL PARISH**

MC=Marston Culy
WM=Wavers Marston
HB= Hill Bickenhill
MB=Middle Bickenhill
CB=Church Bickenhill
LY=Lyndon

————————— Rivers
— — — — — Boundaries,Manors,Parishes.
● Manors in Domesday Survey.

The manors and parishes in and around Solihull Metropolitan Borough.

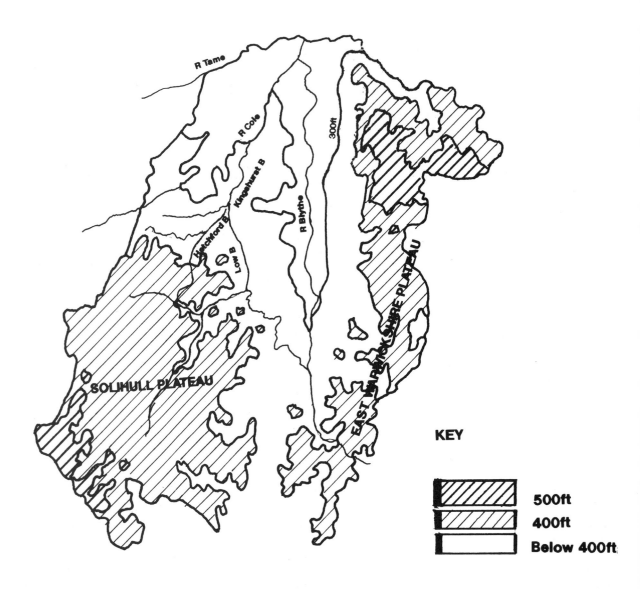

Relief Map of the Solihull area.

Earth's Huge Fabric

The Metropolitan Borough of Solihull lies in the central Midlands, in the old county of Warwickshire and deep within Arden. The countryside is gently undulating, varying in height between 275ft and 550ft, the higher ground in the east and west. In the east, Meriden, Berkswell and Balsall lie at the western edge of the East Warwickshire Plateau while in the west and southwest, Olton, Solihull, Shirley, Knowle and Dorridge lie on the Solihull Plateau.

The two plateaux are separated by the wide valley of the River Blythe which, prone to flooding, meanders northwards through the Borough, collecting many small streams along the way. Beyond Coleshill it unites with the River Cole, then flows on to join the River Tame; ultimately, *via* the Trent and Humber, it enters the North Sea. The Cole forms the western boundary of the Borough for a short way near Majors Green, then passes into Birmingham, re-entering Solihull at Kingshurst. At Chelmsley Wood the Cole is joined by Kingshurst Brook, formed by the union of Hatchford and Low Brooks.

Except in the east the underlying rock of the Borough is almost wholly Keuper Marl within which are occasional small beds of Upper Keuper (Arden) sandstone. Laid down in the Triassic Period the Keuper Marl produces a stiff cold clay soil difficult to work and the natural home of deciduous woodland: ash, hazel and particularly oak. This vast area of heavily wooded country, known from Celtic times as Arden, is crucial to the history of the area.

Between Copt Heath and Barston there is a large patch of Lower Lias (Rhaetic) rock of the Jurassic period containing black shales, grey marl and limestone of marine origin; there are also fossils of bivalves. The resulting soil of limestone and clay is heavy and ill-drained; in the 18th and 19th centuries it was dug and burnt for lime.

In the Meriden/Berkswell area, at a fault line known as the Meriden-Norton Lindsay fault, the geology of the Borough dramatically changes. To the west of the fault the rocks are Triassic but to the east, on the East Warwickshire Plateau, they are older, of the Carboniferous period — Tile Hill Mudstone and Coventry Sandstone. Workable coal lies beneath the area, which the Coal Board wishes to extract by sinking a mine about 3,000 feet deep at Hawkhurst Moor, Berkswell, if planning permission can be obtained.

Also in the Meriden/Berkswell area are small outcrops of Bromsgrove (Keuper) Sandstone. All the sandstones found in the Borough have in the past been quarried for use in local buildings although they do not always weather well. They vary in colour from grey, grey-green through buff to brown and shades of pink. The Keuper clay has also been used; bricks and tiles of varying warm rose hues have been produced over the centuries from numerous small local brick-fields.

Overlying the bedrock of the district — Keuper Marl, Sandstone and Tile Hill Mudstone — are patches of drift: Boulder clay, sand and gravel and silt strewn across the landscape during the Ice Age by the movement of glaciers and ice sheets and by their melt-waters. The soils of the drift are lighter and more porous than the cold clays, and support less heavy tree growth, birch rather than oak, and more shrubs and bushes, creating natural clearings within the woodland.

The Boulder clay, which frequently produces a sandy pebbly soil, lies mostly in the south of the Borough. There are large patches in the Shirley area, at Blossomfield, Four Ashes, Chadwick End, Fen End and Balsall. The sand and gravel is more widely spread; in addition to many small patches throughout the Borough there are extensive areas at Shirley, Knowle, Copt Heath, Bradnocks Marsh, to the north of the National Exhibition Centre (NEC) and at Meriden where, in several places, gravel is being extracted. In addition there is a large patch at Solihull, extending from Sharmans Cross to Catherine de Barnes and including the town centre and Lode Heath.

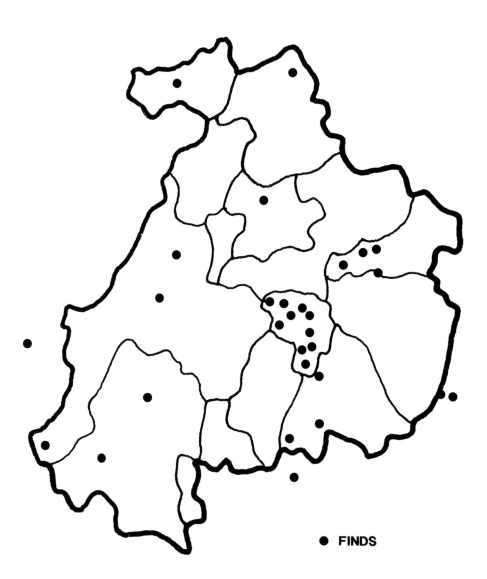

● **FINDS**

The sites of finds — Old Stone Age to Roman — in the Solihull area.

24

A Rude, Unpolish'd Race

It used to be thought that Arden was an 'empty quarter', where no early people ever set foot. While it is true that its damp oak woodland was not attractive to prehistoric man, except for hunting, it is now appreciated that the whole area was not thickly carpeted with trees. Recent finds and research suggest that Stone-Age people, nomadic hunter-gatherers, did frequent the area, living on fruit and berries and what they could catch by fishing and hunting with their flint-tipped arrows and spears. The recent discovery of numerous flints at Barston and Eastcote shows that Mesolithic (Middle Stone Age) people were active there about 8,000 BC. They lived in temporary camps beside the Blythe and other streams, working the flints to produce tools such as scrapers, leaving the waste flakes and cores behind when they moved on. Nearby at Temple Balsall an old Stone Age, roughly flaked, Aucheulian flint hand-axe was discovered in a gravel pit close to the river, the oldest artefact found in the Borough.

Neolithic (New Stone Age: 4,500-2,000 BC) finds include a 'Thames Pick' — a 10 inches long flint tool with a tranchet-shaped point — found at Gorse Farm, Marston Green, and a short-necked beaker recovered from a gravel pit at Meriden. At Long Meadow Farm, Burton Green, Berkswell numerous flint flakes and arrowheads of a slightly later date, Neolithic-Bronze Age (2,400-2,000 BC) have been found. Similar finds were also made at Cheswick Green, and in a wood at Forshaw Heath, while close by at Earlswood a slate perforated whetstone was unearthed.

The people of the Bronze Age (2,400-750 BC) were competent farmers, able to clear tree growth and work the lighter soils of the river terraces and woodland clearings with their bronze tools. A bronze looped palstave — a chisel-edged implement used as a hoe or spade — has been found at Burton Green close to the flint finds. This may have been a Bronze Age farm settlement, possibly in continuous occupation ever since. At Norton Green, Knowle, a bronze axe, dated about 1,300 BC, was found in a cottage garden in 1971. It had probably been lost, but a hoard of four bronze swords discovered at Meriden was probably buried for safe-keeping. Mounds of burnt stones found close to streams in two places at Barston and in New Falling Coppice, Forshaw suggest that Bronze Age settlements were close by. Used either for heating water for cooking or to produce steam for an early type of sauna bath, these stones have been dated to about 1,000 BC.

The Celtic people who entered Britain from the seventh century BC knew how to smelt iron and were able to produce cheap and durable tools. Consequently, during the Iron Age (750 BC-40 AD) man's ability as a farmer greatly increased and considerable areas of woodland were converted to farmland. A warlike people, the Celts occupied tribal areas and, for self-defence, banded together in or near strategically placed camps or hill-forts. The lands of the three tribes: the Coritani, the Dobunni and the Cornovii met in the central Midlands. The former, who probably controlled the upper Avon valley, rarely built forts and of the several in the region Oldbury and Corley were probably of the Cornovii while those in the Lapworth area — Harborough Banks, Barnmoor Wood, Beausale — and the camp at Berry Mound, which lies at the edge of the Borough, possibly belonged to the Dobunni. On a low-lying hill on the eastern bank of the Cole, the multiple ramparts of

Berry Mound enclosed an 11-acre oval site. A permanent settlement during the first century BC, the banks of the hill-fort were much destroyed during the 19th century and the outer two are no longer visible from the ground.

Recent field work at Meriden near Gravel Pit Plantation has revealed ring ditches and a possible Iron Age field system. Close by at The Somers, following the sighting in aerial photographs of interesting crop marks, three juxtaposed overlapping enclosures were discerned and a trial excavation took place. Two of the enclosures are thought to be the sites of Roman marching camps and the third a prehistoric farmstead. The latter, polygonal in shape, underlies the Roman ditch and is thus earlier. As yet undated, it is possibly Iron Age.

The Romans established three major roads: Watling Street, Fosse Way, Ryknild Street, through the Midlands and there are indications that several others existed. Indeed, the marching camps at Meriden may have been an overnight safe resting place along a road from the Roman camp at Metchley (close to the Queen Elizabeth Hospital, Birmingham) to the Lunt Fort at Bagington, near Coventry. A recent major find is a second century AD Roman temple and bath house at Grimstock Hill, Coleshill, thought to have been on a road postulated between Metchley and Mancetter on Watling Street. Such a road would have passed through Castle Bromwich, where Stone and Bronze Age material, an Iron Age coin of the Brigantes, and a Roman coin of Faustina II have been found, as have traces of Roman buildings in the Castle bailey. On a promontory overlooking an ancient major crossing of the Tame, Castle Bromwich occupied an important defensive position.

The Romans were clearly active within the Borough; a landscape survey at Barston has revealed Roman pottery sherds in several places and a Romano-British settlement and field system near Eastcote. Sherds of *mortaria* (mixing bowls) found close to Solihull station suggest a similar settlement existed within a half-mile radius. Roman coins have been found in Lyndon Road, Olton, at Norton Green (in the same garden as the bronze axe) and at Chessetts Wood, where a hoard of brass coins of the third century AD, and weighing 15lbs, were turned up by the plough in 1778.

In 411 Roman rule in Britain ceased abruptly; the Romanised way of life totally collapsed. There were no new coins, no pottery and within two generations many technical skills were lost. In this post-Roman period the population, of possibly two to three million, lived in the countryside, maintained by subsistence farming. They managed to keep the land open and there is no evidence of regeneration of woodland, large amounts of which the Romans had cleared, until the sixth century.

About 450 the Anglo-Saxons began arriving in Britain and gradually spread westwards. They found the prime land occupied by the post-Roman British and, it is now thought, settled beside them amicably. Ultimately the two peoples merged. The number of immigrants was never large, perhaps tens of thousands, yet it was the Anglo-Saxon language, law and culture which became paramount, almost certainly with the acquiescence of the British population.

By the sixth century the Anglo-Saxons were settled in the central Midlands, evidence having been found beside the Fosse Way and on the gravel terraces of the Trent and Avon and their tributaries. Later they entered Arden where place-name evidence suggests their own earliest settlements had Anglo-Saxon names ending in *tun* (ton), meaning 'settlement, estate, village', indicating the area was open, already free of trees, either naturally or having been cleared by earlier people. Marston [Green], Hampton [in Arden], Kineton [Green] and Barston fall into this category; all lie below 400 feet on spurs or knolls of drift and close to at least two good streams. Marston (earliest form *Merstone*) means 'marsh settlement' but the village was carefully sited above the danger of flooding. Hampton (*Hantone*) meaning 'high village' is situated on a knoll above Shadow Brook and the Blythe, while Kineton (*Cinctun*) meaning 'King's estate', now to be equated with Kineton Green Road, occupies a ridge between Kineton Brook and Hatchford Brook. Barston must have had a pre-Anglo-Saxon name, stemming from its Romano-British occupants, who made the field system at Eastcote and cultivated it, possibly for centuries.

26

Recent research suggests that villages with names ending in *tun* were taken over by the Anglo-Saxons between 750 and 950 as were those with names ending in ley (*leah*). Ulverley (*Ulverlei*) meaning 'the clearing of Wolfhere', belongs to this group, the ley ending indicating the village was situated in a clearing and that beyond lay deep woodland, for considerable areas of well-wooded country still remained in Arden, particularly on the clay lands above 400 feet. Ulverley, now to be equated with Olton, was a parent of Solihull.

Other Anglo-Saxons settled at Elmdon (*Elmedone*) meaning 'hill of the elms', at Longdon (*Langedone*) meaning 'long hill' and at [Hill] Bickenhill (*Bichehelle*) meaning 'projecting hill', the situation of all three being reflected in their names. Recent place-name evidence suggests that settlements with *dun* (don) name-endings were founded earlier than those with 'hill' endings and that *dun* means 'a hill with a flat top suitable for a settlement site'. This was certainly the case at Longdon (also a parent of Solihull), the village being sited in the Marsh Lane/Yew Tree Lane/Hampton Lane area of Solihull. Hampton Lane follows the whale-back shape of the 'long hill' and divided Longdon's communally worked fields: Seed Furlong (*Sydefurlong*) to the north and Hain Field (*Hemfeld*), Berry Field (*Burifeld*) and Wheatcroft (*Watcroft*) to the south, the land falling away to the common meadows beside the Blythe.

All these settlements were sited on islands of drift, some of which were quite small. Yet these seem to have been preferred for, where the drift patches were extensive, the villages were established at the edge, presumably because the soil at the centre was often poor.

Springs and sweet water were important; at Berkswell (*Berchewelle*) meaning 'spring associated with a man called Beorcol', five rise together, which may have inspired a degree of veneration. They feed a well near the church used daily until the 1940s and still described by geologists as a 'strong spring'. Adjoining Berkswell is Alspath (*Ailespede*), meaning 'Aelle's path' and now known as Meriden. The Anglo-Saxon settlement was on the hill above the present village and beside the 'path' (meaning 'road across heathland') to Allesley, to which the first element may refer.

The settlement of Arden was slow; how slow may be gauged by the Domesday Survey taken in 1086, at least three centuries after the Anglo-Saxons entered the district.

The survey records that there were 13 manors within what is now Greater Solihull: Elmedone, Cintone, Hantone, Ailespede, Merstone, Ulverlei, Langedone plus two manors within Bichehelle, two within Bercestone and two within Berchewelle. [Castle] Bromwich was then part of Aston manor and Chelmsley Wood and Kingshurst part of Coleshill.

The Domesday population was small, 11 of the manors together having a total of 82 families. Ulverley and Hampton had larger populations with 29 and 70 families respectively; each also had a priest and presumably a simple church. Both manors were extensive, Ulverley extending from Coventry Road to Alcester Road and including what is now Solihull town, while Hampton had several outlying daughter settlements, including Diddington, Balsall, Knowle, Nuthurst and Baddesley [Clinton], which almost certainly originated as summer grazing camps. Later they became permanent settlements. Several Avon Valley and south Warwickshire manors had similar grazing dependencies in Arden, Packwood being a daughter of Wasperton and Tanworth [in Arden], of Brailes.

The survey also records the number of plough lands in each manor, that is the amount of land prepared for cultivation, as well as the number of plough teams available. Each team was estimated to be able to work 120 acres of land. Thus at Kineton, according to the survey, there was arable land available for two ploughs *ie* 240 acres. The five families who lived there owned two plough teams between them and were accordingly able to cultivate all the land. Within Hampton manor and its daughter settlements 22 plough lands, that is 2,640 acres, were available for cultivation but there were only 15 plough teams; 13 were worked by the 66 village families and two by the serf families who farmed the demesne (home farm) for the new Norman lord of the manor, Geoffrey de Wirce. Thus some 800 acres were prepared but uncultivated, perhaps awaiting the acquisition of further plough teams as part of a programme of expansion, or possibly taken out of cultivation by de Wirce to enclose as a park. Altogether in the 13 manors there were some 10,000 acres prepared for arable crops (a quarter of the acreage of the present Borough) and 54 plough teams available.

Beyond the pockets of arable lay more than 30,000 acres of land, much of it covered with trees, for the survey also records (in leagues and furlongs) the extent of the woodland. It has been determined that one Domesday league equals 12 furlongs, one square furlong equalling 10 acres, thus in the cluster of manors close to Hatchford Brook, Low Brook and the Lower Blythe — Marston, Elmdon, the Bickenhills, the Barstons and Longdon — the area of woodland recorded was small, less than 2,000 acres altogether. But in the other manors, most of which were larger and on higher ground, the woodland was extensive: more than 2,500 acres each at Alspath, Ulverley and Kineton, 1,400 acres at Berkswell and 13,000 acres at Hampton, although much of this was probably within the daughter settlements.

Before the Conquest each manor had been held freely by an Anglo-Saxon. The famous Countess Godiva held Alspath and her grandson, Earl Edwin of Mercia, Ulverley and Aston. Turchil, another important local man, held Hampton, Kineton, and one of the Barston manors, his father, Alwin, holding the other; Coleshill belonged to the King.

Those who opposed William the Conqueror and fought at Hastings had their lands confiscated, but those who were absent and submitted were excused. Earl Edwin, fighting in the north in October 1066, retained his lands until his death in 1072, despite occasional rebellious outbursts. Aston then passed to the King, and Ulverley was given to Princess Cristina (a member of the Saxon Royal house), probably as a gesture of goodwill. King William rewarded his followers and friends with grants of many manors. Turchil was a quisling who supported him; after 1066 he lost Hampton, Barston and Kineton manors but received instead Marston, both Bickenhills, Elmdon, Longdon, his father's manor of Barston and many others. By 1086 he was a major landowner, holding 70 of the 279 manors in Warwickshire, many of which he granted to under-tenants.

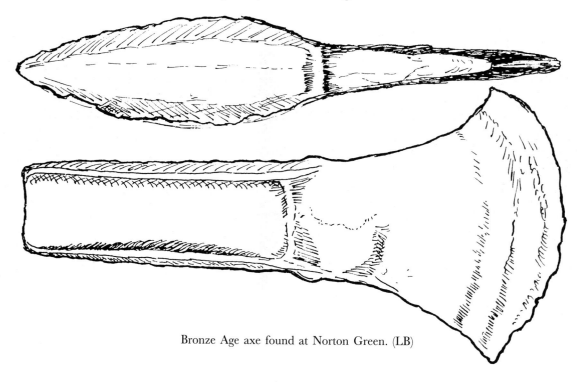

Bronze Age axe found at Norton Green. (LB)

28

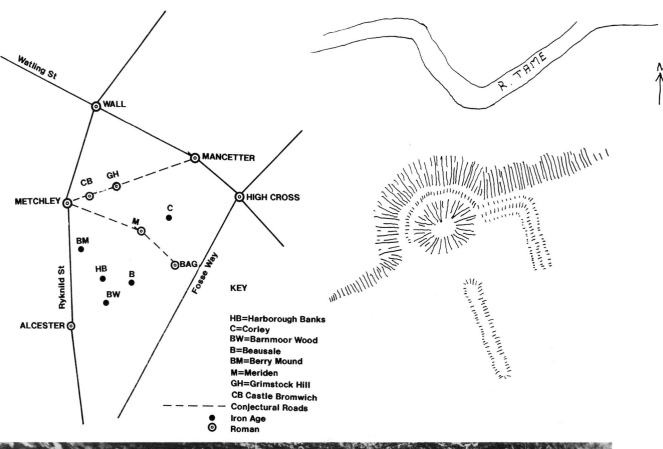

KEY

HB=Harborough Banks
C=Corley
BW=Barnmoor Wood
B=Beausale
BM=Berry Mound
M=Meriden
GH=Grimstock Hill
CB Castle Bromwich
– – – Conjectural Roads
● Iron Age
◎ Roman

LEFT: Iron Age forts, Roman roads and sites in the Central Midlands.
RIGHT: Castle Bromwich Mound, now almost wholly destroyed. BELOW:
The Well, Berkswell, late 19th century. (SL)

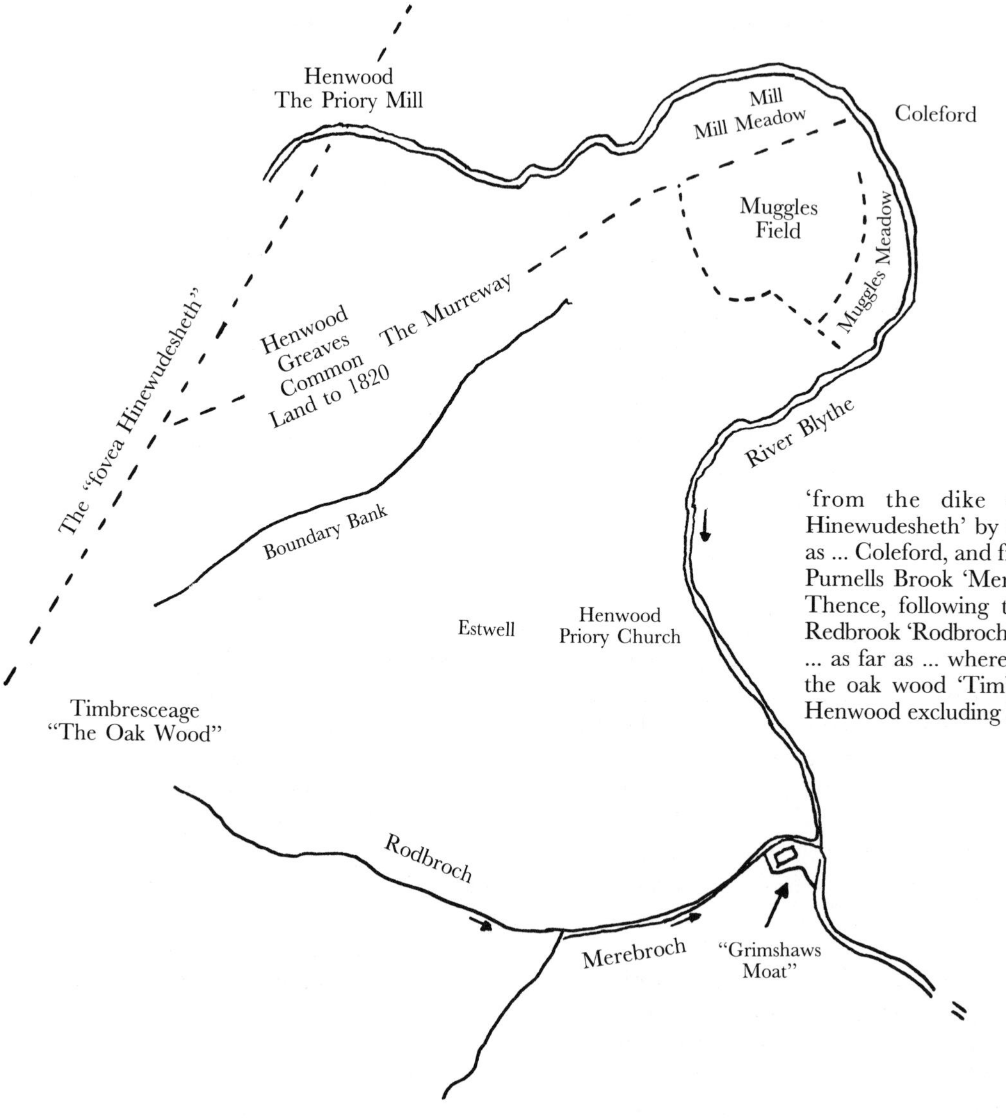

Henwood
The Priory Mill
Mill
Mill Meadow
Coleford
Muggles
Field
Muggles Meadow
The "fovea Hinewudesheth"
Henwood
Greaves
Common
Land to 1820
The Murreway
River Blythe
Boundary Bank
Estwell
Henwood
Priory Church
Timbresceage
"The Oak Wood"
Rodbroch
Merebroch
"Grimshaws
Moat"

'from the dike of Henwood Heath 'fov
Hinewudesheth' by the miry way 'Murrewey' as f
as ... Coleford, and from the ford ... as far as ... whe
Purnells Brook 'Merebroch' runs into ... the Blyth
Thence, following the bank ... as far as ... whe
Redbrook 'Rodbroch' runs into Merebroch and then
... as far as ... where the stream rises. Then throu
the oak wood 'Timbresceage' as far as the dike
Henwood excluding Muggles Field 'Muchelingewicl

Map and extract from the Charter of Henwood Priory defining the boundary of the land granted by Ketelberne. (LB)

From the Rural Landscape Learn

In the post-Domesday period the national population began to rise and by the 14th century had trebled. In places land shortage was a problem, but in Arden there was ample for those with the energy and drive to exploit it. After 1086 the area was a hive of activity as trees were felled and new fields, farms and parks created.

During these years Hampton's daughter settlements — Diddington, Knowle, Balsall, Nuthurst, Baddesley Clinton — became independent manors, as did Castle Bromwich and the dependencies of Packwood and Tanworth. Other offshoot settlements were also established, including Middle Bickenhill, Lyndon, Wavers Marston, Meriden and Solihull.

In the main, each settlement had a separate open-field unit, invariably a complexity of fields and furlongs, yet it is a particular characteristic of Arden that much of its expansion was by individual effort resulting in many independent farms. Such farms or assarts were the work of one man and his family who acquired an area of land from the manorial lord which they then brought into cultivation. The farm boundary was usually marked by an embanked hedge and ditch and often the homestead was moated, at least 50 moated sites being known in Greater Solihull. Such tenants were free and not bound by feudal obligations such as labour service and special taxes and fines.

Many overlords encouraged the development of their estates and the income it generated; others granted their manors away. Princess Cristina gave all her possessions, including Ulverley, to the de Limesi family, she herself becoming a nun. The lands of Count Meulan passed to the Earls of Warwick as did most of those of Turchil; however, his manor of Longdon was retained by his son, Siward, who granted it to one Ketelberne; Catherine de Barnes is a distorted modern variation of his name.

About 1160 Ketelberne gave some 170 acres of land in Longdon, near a spring at Estwell in the north-east corner of the manor, to found a priory for Benedictine nuns. Dedicated to St Margaret it became known as Henwood Priory, its bounds being clearly defined.

In the mediaeval period, giving land to a religious house was an investment for the afterlife, an insurance policy for the souls of the grantor and his family. Many privileges were granted to the nuns at Henwood; they had their own manor court, permission to cut timber for their buildings and to erect a water-mill. Their church and moated house stood a little to the east of the present Henwood Hall, their mill being on the site of the present Henwood Mill. Between it and Henwood lay *Hinewudesheth* (Henwood Heath) and beyond, Copt Heath, both extensive areas of common land or waste. From the many wood names it is clear that Henwood was originally well-wooded, the Heath (and many other heaths locally) probably being created by the constant grazing of the underwood and saplings. Many trees would remain but not regenerate; regenerating woodland (often called groves) had to be protected by a ditch and bank.

Elsewhere in Longdon a new demesne was established, well away from the parent village. The moated manor house, the site of Longdon Hall, lay at the heart of about 180 acres, now chiefly occupied by the golf course and bounded by Lady Byron Lane, Longdon Road, Purnells Brook and Warwick Road. Much of the rest of the manor was granted by Ketelberne and his successors to individuals for assarts. At least 10 independent farms, possibly more, were established in this way at Longdon. Eight which had moated homesteads may be identified: Malvern Hall (home of the de Malverne family); Berry Hall (de Buri family); Ravenshaw Hall; Moat House (Salemon family); Widney Farm, now The Chase; Widney Manor Farm (de Aylesbury family); Tilehouse Green, Browns Lane; Bentley Farm, Mill Lane. Adjoining The Chase, Henwood Priory had further land known as Southey (*hai* meaning enclosure) granted to them c1250. Later Widney became a sub-manor of Longdon.

Longdon was a typical Arden manor, having a core of open-fields with common meadows, a separate demesne, numerous severalty farms with moated homesteads, and extensive common and waste including Catherine de Barnes and Bentley Heath.

In the adjoining manor of Ulverley the de Limesi family established a new settlement at Solihull on top of the 'miry hill'. Intended as a trading centre, the town was carefully planted at the crossing of two important roads: from Birmingham to Warwick, and from Worcester to Coventry, the latter following, in places, an ancient saltway. The potential settlers were offered building plots in the already laid out streets, where they could erect a home-cum-workshop to suit their trade. As an incentive the de Limesi's offered burgage tenure: in return for a money rent the tenant was free, at liberty to direct his own life and affairs without feudal obligations and interference. For the manorial lord there were tolls and fines from the weekly Wednesday market held in The Square, and a higher rent return than from land under cultivation. Solihull succeeded; by 1190 it was included in a tax list, a church was built and by c1200 Ulverley was being referred to as the Old Town or Olton. Solihull became pre-eminent: a town with a Royal Charter for a market and annual three-day Fair by 1242, a manor, a parish.

The land beyond the town developed in a similar way to Longdon. There was a core of communal fields — *le chirchefeld, crabbewallefeld, orchardesfeld, bromfild* — beside the Warwick Road, but much of the land was developed as severalty farms. The de Buckemor family established a farm with moated homestead — *Buckemorestede*, later Moat Farm — beside Moat Lane; by 1290 the Libers were at *Libereslond* (Libbards Farm) and the Blosmeville family were in the Blossomfield Road/Danford Lane area, while the moated house of the Madur family, Maidens Bower, occupied the site of Dorchester Road. There were other private farms at Whiteley (Malvern Park Farm); Whitefields Road (Garardes); Hillfield (Hall); Widney Lane (Blakestede and Abel Farm); Longmore Road; Streetsbrook Road (Longgele and Silhill Hall), and Lovelace Avenue (Haiteley), not all being moated. The largest and most important homestead was Hobs Moat, recently excavated. Here the d'Oddingsell family, who succeeded the de Limesi's as the manorial lords of Solihull, had their fine stone house. Built in the early 13th century it was later remodelled and improved to reflect the status of William d'Oddingsell II as a great soldier, Constable of Ireland, husband of a lady of Royal blood and friend of the King. The house platform was surrounded by large internal and external banks which exaggerate the depth and width of the vallum. Antiquarian Sir William Dugdale thought that beyond the moat there was a deer park 'at least a mile in diameter'. By 1320 the male d'Oddingsells were all dead, the manor sold and Hobs Moat ceased to be important.

The farms were divided from each other by heaths: Dickens, Elmdon, Fulford, Grange, Leewode (Lode), Shirley, Turtelmass, the moats often sited at the heath's edge.

Beyond the town were the three settlements of Olton, Shirley and Shelly. At Olton lived the remnants of the Ulverley population which slowly declined while Solihull grew. It was included within the extensive parish of Solihull as was Longdon, the people of both places being drawn to the new town at the expense of their home villages. At Shirley there were a few houses and an inn strung out along the Stratford Road, here called Shirley Street. The inhabitants farmed, grazing their animals on the heath, and serving travellers passing through. At Shelly there was a thriving hamlet on the then Kings Highway from Solihull to Henley. This road joined the Stratford

Road, here called Monkspath Street, at Monkspath Bridge, erected by 1339. The land was farmed communally, there were at least two commercial fish-pools and a water-mill on the Blythe, the many meatless days decreed by the church making the farming of bream, roach, tench, pike and perch a profitable business. A series of bad harvests, starting in 1312 and culminating in the great famine of 1315-7, in which half Europe starved and thousands died, undoubtedly effected Arden. Fish must then have been a valuable food and the number of local fish farms may have increased as a result.

A generation later a terrible plague, the Black Death, spread across England, reaching the Midlands in the spring of 1349, killing perhaps a quarter of the national population. Further outbreaks in 1360, 1369 and 1374 continued the devastation and by 1377 half the people in the country are thought to have died. Henceforth the community at Shelly (and others elsewhere) appears to have declined, the established family names disappearing and the open-fields being enclosed. By 1500 there were few residents, the mill had ceased, the fisheries gone and the hamlet was known as Shelly Green.

At Shelly, Solihull and Tanworth parishes abutted; the latter contained several estates, and the manor of Monkspath, granted to Roger de Ulehale by the Earl of Warwick before 1184. Within Monkspath independent farms developed, it being possible to trace those with moated homesteads: Sidenhales Farm; Mancetters Moat (by Junction 4 of the M42); Light Hall (La Lych); Elliott's Hall; Crouenhales Moat (both in Creynolds Lane), and The Mount (Cheswick). The latter had a double moat and was probably the Ulehale's manor house. The east moat was fortified c1300 with banks and ditches but apparently never used; twice excavated, the site has produced scant evidence of its past. Along streams feeding the Blythe, commercial fish-pools were made, as at Shelly, basically by damming a valley and creating a by-pass to divert flood water round the pond. There were six pools within Monkspath: Old Betlesworth (near Jerrings Hall), Totlemoss (now Woodloes Estate), Cleobury, at Benetford Mill (off Salter Street), Elliott's Hall, and the largest, Illshaw Pool (near Sidenhales Farm), which covered 10 acres and had a dam 220 yards long. In 1317 Henry de Sidenhale was paid £13 16s 8d for fish from this great pool, equivalent to the income of a large estate.

The manor of Alspath followed a similar pattern to Ulverley and Solihull. The original hilltop village (where the church stands) was superseded in importance by a later settlement, Meriden, meaning 'pleasant valley', which grew up on flatter ground beside the important mediaeval road from London to Chester. The new village had its own open-fields and ample grazing on Meriden Heath but trade, particularly travellers, appears to have been the chief occupation over the centuries and there were several inns. A charter for a weekly Tuesday market and an eight-day annual Fair at the feast of St Lawrence (10 August) was acquired in 1318, presumably to be held on Meriden Green. Beyond the village, much of the land was developed as severalty farms some of which — Walsh Hall, the home of the Walshe family, and Marlbrook, named from the nearby stream (now Pickford Brook) — became sub-manors.

In places Meriden still retains its ancient landscape: deep, narrow, winding lanes, hidden farms and moats, embanked hedges marking the boundaries of the mediaeval assarts. There remain several parcels of ancient woodland — Boultbees, Church, Chantry, Meigh's, Meriden Shafts, Millisons, Crow Woods — deliberately preserved by enclosing them by bank and ditch.

Having inherited Berkswell manor from his brother, Count Meulan, Henry, Earl of Warwick granted it in 1123 to the Mundeville family. By 1166 they had enclosed about 250 acres of woodland with a ditch and high earth bank to create a deer park — the grounds to Berkswell Hall — for their special use. The bank, which is still traceable, would have been topped by a stout oak fence or pale to keep the animals in and poachers out. Venison was greatly prized and poaching at Berkswell is recorded in 1322 and 1366 when hare, rabbit, pheasant, partridge and fish as well as deer were taken. A keeper or parker cared for the park, this worthwhile office being granted to Richard de Helegh, one of the King's archers, in 1397. The site of the parker's lodge is unknown but it was probably on raised ground commanding a view of the park. In 1456 it needed repair: '1,000 tiles, 6½ doz gutter tiles, doz "crestez", pay of tilers, Total 12s 9d'. Made primarily for a managed supply of game including wild boar, native deer, and the newly introduced fallow deer and rabbit, mediaeval parks were pleasant places to ride, hawk and shoot. They also preserved trees which until recent times have always been regarded as a valuable crop.

At Berkswell, as at Meriden, areas of woodland were intentionally conserved and worked by coppicing to produce a useful income. Some 41 acres of ancient woodland, Rough Close Wood, still survive to the south of Hawkhurst Moor. Enclosed on the north and northeast by a particularly large bank and 24 feet wide ditch, probably mediaeval, the wood was originally larger. After 10 acres of 'Ruffe Close' were sold c1546, 150 perches of new bank and ditch were made at a cost of 50s together with five gates costing 6s 8d; this may be the present southern boundary of the wood where the bank is smaller and the ditch only 15 feet wide. If the projected mine is permitted this living archaeological monument will be destroyed, as will Hawkhurst Moor, once an open heath known in 1275 as *le hauekerismore* meaning 'marsh of the hawker'.

Berkswell, like Longdon, Solihull, Tanworth and Alspath, was chiefly developed as private farms, seven moated sites being traceable: at Ram Hall; Burton Green; The Moat; Moat House Farm; Barriesplace near Beechwood; near Reeves Green; near Sunnyside Farm. Situated mostly in the centre of the parish the farms are separated from each other by numerous narrow twisting lanes, which meet at small greens: Benton, Eaves, Reeves, Carol. These are probably the remnants of heaths, the latter being known as *le Carnewilleheth* in 1278. Of Berkswell's open-fields, no obvious trace remains but from field-name evidence (*eg* shutt, flat) small units were probably situated at Beanit; off Back Lane; near Lavender Hall; and at Oldnall End. At the edge of the parish there was an extensive area of waste, Berkswell Common, available for common grazing, as were Hawkhurst Moor, Beechwood Common and Bradnocks Marsh.

In the northwest corner of Berkswell is the separate manor of Mercote, meaning 'marsh dwelling'. It may have been the site of Berkswell's second Domesday manor held by Walter in 1086. The de Mercote family owned the estate in 1163 and until it was sold to John Botrye in 1384. It passed by marriage to John Mathew, a Coventry skinner, in 1465 and remained in this family for 300 years. Mercote Hall, an extremely ancient timber-framed building with enormous beams, thick walls and surrounded by a wide moat, was probably built by the de Mercotes. In the 18th century, when it was acquired by the Eardley Wilmot family, the house was completely encased in brick; it was demolished in 1926.

Bordered by the Blythe and crossed by other streams, Mercote had two water-mills, one on the river and a second, with an enormous pool, close to the Hall. Fish farming almost certainly formed part of the estate economy, Thomas Boter supplying bream for the restocking of the pools at Baddesley Clinton Hall after they had been overhauled and repaired in 1448. Above Bradnocks Mill is a riverside field called 'Stew', which probably adjoined the site of the keep fish-pond in the river.

ABOVE: Old Berry Hall, recently restored after years of neglect, still stands within its moat. From 1505 to 1671 it was the home of the Catholic Waring family. (JW) RIGHT: Henwood Watermill, a late 18th century building on an ancient site. Milling continued into the 1930s. (WCRO) BELOW: Moat Farm, Moat Lane, now the site of the Council Depôt. (DG)

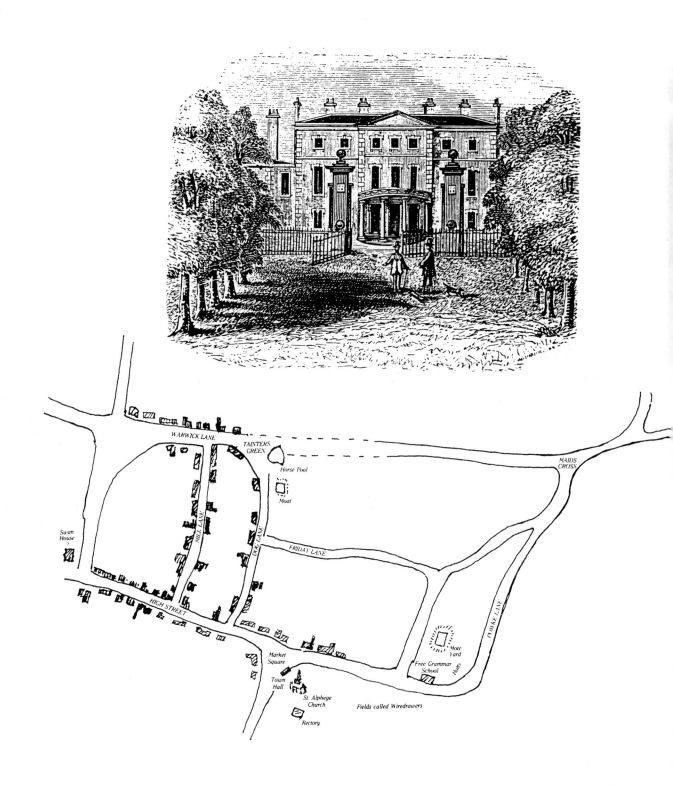

ABOVE: Malvern Hall in 1863; begun in 1702, it was enlarged c1780 to designs by the architect Sir John Soane. The moated house was nearer Marsh Lane. BELOW: A conjectural map of Solihull Town in the 17th century. (KJS)

LEFT: Libbards Farm, an 18th century house now divided into flats and surrounded by an estate. The earlier moated homestead was near Widney Manor Station. (SL) RIGHT: Whitley *alias* Malvern Park Farm, Widney Manor Road, early this century. (SL) BELOW: Bentley Manor Farm, Mill Lane, Bentley Heath, demolished in the 1960s and replaced by Dorridge Methodist Church. (TG)

At the MOUNT COTTAGE.   FARM – SHIRLEY.

EX MONTE ALTO.

ABOVE: Silhill Hall, Streetsbrook Road, a fine mediaeval house, demolished illegally by its owner in 1966. (SL) BELOW: The moated site, known as The Mount at Cheswick Green, was used in the early 1900s as a pleasure garden. Whether it was quite as successful as this advert suggests is doubtful. (SL)

LEFT: Mercote Hall, Berkswell, was used to house German prisoners-of-war from 1915-18. After they left, the building remained unoccupied until demolished in 1926. (SL) RIGHT: The Church and Church Farm on the hill-top settlement of Alspath (Meriden). (JW) BELOW: The children of Meriden cluster round the market cross which traditionally marks the centre of England. c1910 (WF)

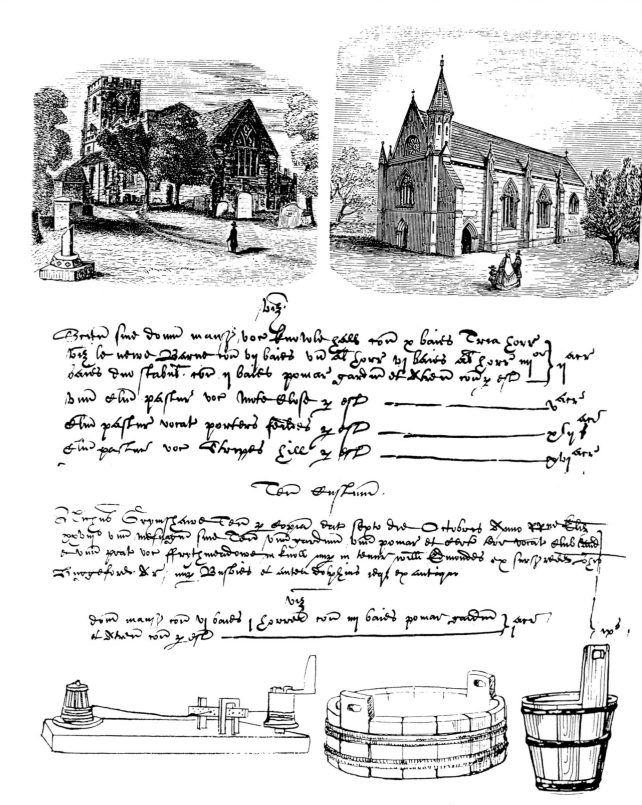

LEFT: Hampton-in-Arden Church c1863. Until 1643 it had a tall spire which fell during a violent storm. RIGHT: Temple Balsall Church c1863. CENTRE: Two extracts from a survey of Knowle c1605 describing: a) Knowle Hall, its barns, stables and lands; b) the property of Nicholas Grimshaw. (LB) BELOW: LEFT: A simple wire-drawing machine. RIGHT: A wooden bucket and tub, two examples of coopery.

Heifers Graze, or Buxom Damsels Ted

Across the Blythe from Mercote lies Hampton, held in the 12th century by the de Arden family, granted to them by the Mowbrays to whom it had passed. The de Ardens, related to Turchil, were important locally and considerable landowners. Beside the church, begun by Geoffrey de Wirce about 1150, was their moated manor house (now called Moat House) and park where Sir Hugh Arden spent much time. In 1251 he obtained a Royal charter for a weekly Tuesday market, held on the green beside the church, and a three-day fair on the eve, day and morrow of St Luke, 18 October.

Sir Hugh's son, William, inherited Hampton but was often absent for he supported Simon de Montfort and in 1265 fought against the King at Evesham; Simon was killed, his followers scattered. William was pardoned and reputedly went on a crusade. In 1276, on Friday 17 April, in a dispute over money, he was murdered in his grove at Henwood by Richard de Buri, presumably of Berry Hall. An inventory of William's property, taken by 15 local gentlemen, reveals that he owned land worth £7 in several local villages, worth £5 12s 8d at Longdon and £23 13s 6¾d at Knowle, where he was lord of the manor. At Hampton his manor house had two gardens and a vineyard; there were also two parks, one near the house and another at Castle Hills in Bickenhill parish. In the demesne were 460 acres of arable land worth 4d per acre, meadow, fenced pasture and a hayfield. On the Blythe were two water-mills worth £2 3s 0d per annum and a great fish-trap worth 6s 8d per annum. Other income came from market profits and stall fees, the sale of underwood and pannage (the right to pasture pigs in the woods); everything was valued.

Early settled and below 400ft, Hampton appears to have developed almost wholly as an open-field village with few assarts and, apart from the manor house, only one moated homestead, Walford Hall. The 11 known communally-worked fields lay around the village and park, with several common meadows beside the streams. Pasture for common grazing was available on Hampton, Elmdon and Catherine de Barnes Heaths and there were some patches of wood, perhaps 200 acres in all. Such communal cultivation was often associated with villeinage — being unfree, tied to the manor — and certainly the people of Hampton were chiefly bond tenants, who owed labour service to the manorial lord. This obliged them to work for a number of days per year on the lord's land, ploughing, weeding, sowing, mowing, and at harvest time. Each day's work was valued in pence and in 1276 was worth £4 10s 7d. Most tenants also paid a money rent, the 31 virgates of 'bond land', approximately 900 acres, bringing in £5 12s 5d per annum, although some tenants paid in kind, hens and geese worth 21d being received; in total Hampton was valued at £45 3s 11d.

Diddington in the north-east corner of Hampton was a separate manor with its own open-fields. About 1230 the manor was purchased by the Arden family and from then its descent followed that of Knowle.

Knowle, part of Hampton manor at the time of Domesday, remained a detached portion of Hampton parish until 1850. The first reference to *Gnolle* (a hill) is c1200, when William de Arden of Hampton gave Knowle manor to his wife, Amice. By 1220 the Ardens had a manor house at

Knowle with a chapel for their special use, the village people having to walk to Hampton to church. William de Arden's inventory of 1276 shows that at Knowle, in addition to his house and garden, he had a vinery, 140 acres of arable worth 3d per acre, 20 acres of meadow, underwood and grazing on the waste, worth altogether £4 1s 8d. The manorial water-mill on Cuttle Brook was worth 16s and the 436 acres of land let to bond tenants plus the 'day works' were valued at £8 17s 1¼d. There were also some free tenants, not tied to the manor, paying together in rent £3 7s 5½d. In 1284 Knowle manor was sold to Edward I and Queen Eleanor; when she died he was heartbroken and gave Knowle with 21 other manors to Westminster Abbey, as an endowment to pay for masses for the repose of her soul.

Monastic houses ran their estates efficiently, a bailiff usually acting as manager. With the reeve, who organized the daily business, he ensured that the bond tenants fulfilled their numerous feudal obligations. At Knowle in the 12 months September 1294-5 the bailiff was present for only 20 weeks, the records and accounts being kept by the reeve, Richard ate Milne, a local man probably elected to the post by his fellow tenants. From the rent roll it appears there were fewer free tenants than in 1276 but more bond tenants; there was also a number of smallholders.

Carefully itemized, the accounts show that the demesne arable had been ploughed by six waged ploughmen, but the tenants were obliged to do the winter and spring sowing (89 man days for each sowing) their only recompense being food and drink: bread, cheese, meat and ale in winter and bread, herrings and ale in spring. They also did the mowing (74 man days) and harvesting (432 man days), again their only return being refreshment; the same menu but with home-produced cider at harvest time. On the home farm dairying predominated, a cowherd and daily dairymaid being employed. They made 26½ gallons of butter and 20¼ cwt of cheese which were sold for £3 10s 7½d. Sold too were all the fish in the ponds; these were about to be cleaned out, a major expense at £7. Wheat, oats and 40 animals — oxen, steers, heifers, calves — plus 34 bacon pigs also went to market.

A considerable amount of ditching was done and four oaks felled in the park, William Shortleg being contracted to remove the roots. The timber was needed to build a granary and unloading wharf, three carpenters working on it for 23 weeks and a fourth for 14 weeks; each was paid 6d per week with board and lodging provided. Nothing was wasted; the bark and unwanted branches (called crops) were sold, the proceeds more than meeting the cost of the hinges and large quantity of nails required for the building. Also bought during the year were salt for the larder and the dairy which also needed new buckets, and linen cloth for straining the butter. Rye, beans, white peas, mares, pigs, and oxen were purchased as well. When all was totalled the manor was £22 17s 3d in profit; three brothers from Westminster Abbey travelled to Knowle to collect the money, consuming during their stay bread, ale, oats, four geese, two pullets and two cheeses.

The arable land of the Knowle tenants lay in the common-fields, of which there were several, although some seem to have been divisions within larger fields. Only the exact position of *Heynefilde* (at Heronfield) is known but there appear to have been three or four other units — near the village centres at Chessetts Wood, Knowle Wood, and towards Barston.

Following the Black Death there was a labour shortage. Bond tenants, aware of their value, wished to work where they chose and not for their lord without pay. By 1408 the tenurial arrangements at Knowle had apparently changed to allow for this, although some work obligations remained. These were priced and measured: thus a mowing work obliged a tenant to give a whole day to mowing a given area of the lord's hay for 2d pay. A hay-making work took two days and paid ½d, only harvest work included food and was paid at 2d for three-quarters of a day. For many large landowners it became more profitable to lease out their estates: Coventry Priory leased out Packwood and the Crown leased Berkswell piecemeal until 1557 and then as a whole.

The large manor of Balsall across the Blythe from Knowle was also part of the parish of Hampton until 1863. First recorded early in the 12th century as *Beleshale*, the name-ending suggests that the landscape is one of shallow hollows, and indeed many long narrow gullies cross the area.

Roger de Mowbray, lord of Hampton, gave land in Balsall to the Knights Templar, an order of monk-knights founded in 1118 to protect pilgrims as they travelled through the Holy Land. At Temple Balsall, where they had some 650 acres, they established a Preceptory where a number of brothers lived and ran the estate. They had numerous bond tenants, a water-mill, house and park, and about 1290 built the present church. In 1268 they were granted a charter for a weekly Thursday market and two three-day Fairs on the feasts of St Gregory and St Matthew (12 March and 21 September). The Templars were given much land including the manors of Barston, Sherborne, and Fletchamstead and throughout Christendom they acquired property and great wealth. This caused jealousy in high places; in 1308 the whole order was suppressed, stripped of its possessions and the brothers, including John Coningeston, who had been at Balsall for 36 years, imprisoned. Their property reverted to the donors but in 1322 was given to the Knights Hospitaller of St John of Jerusalem.

The Hospitallers, also an order of monk-knights, sheltered pilgrims in the Holy Land. They administered the Balsall estate profitably; in 1338 120 acres of meadow produced an income of £15, the dovecot 10s, the water-mill £3. The preceptor and his household of two brothers, two chaplains and 10 paid officials and servants lived at the Preceptory, part of which still exists as The Hall. They were allowed per year £15 for bread, £10 for beer and £13 for flesh, fish and other kitchen needs; their clothes were also provided. Balsall remained a Preceptory until the 15th century when the Hospitallers leased the estate to a succession of lay farmers who made their home at The Hall.

A second manor within Balsall, *Chedelesuuich* — Chadwick — meaning 'farm near a spring', was first recorded in the 12th century. Purchased by the Arden family it passed c1298 to John Peche, then lord of Hampton, into which manor it was absorbed. The present Chadwick Manor and park is a modern creation to enhance the Victorian house. Nearby at Netherwood Lodge, Fen End Farm, and Oldwich, meaning old ditch or dike, are moated sites marking the homesteads of mediaeval farms, including that of the Attefenne family, who were first mentioned in 1185.

To the south of Chadwick was Netherwood Heath, and to the east the vast waste of Balsall Common. Until modern times the few inhabitants lived chiefly at its edge in spread settlements: Meer End, Needlers End, Wootton Green, and Balsall Street, where there are indications of a fourth moat. The road through this hamlet was of some importance and there is an ancient inn.

In contrast to Balsall the people of Barston lived in close proximity, their houses ranged along the village street, gable ends facing the road, an ancient alignment. Barston had a considerable area of communally worked land, the core fields including Aldridges (Old ridges), Milfeld, Nipland, Great Field and Tynhill lying close to the village. Other small units existed at Walsal End, Eastcote and Ryton End.

There was common grazing at Barston Park and Escott Wood, and numerous water meadows divided into doles, each portion allotted to a tenant as his share of the communally grown hay. Barston manorial mill, valued at 4s in the Domesday Survey, was on the Blythe at Bradnocks Marsh.

During the mediaeval period Barston manor formed part of the Temple Balsall estate, having been given by the Marmion family, then lords of Barston, to the Knights Templar. It passed to the Knights Hospitaller and in 1388 was managed by a resident bailiff who received an annual salary of 13s 4d. The Barston estate income of £16 1s 8d came from rents (£10), land and stock including pasturing 200 cattle, probably at Piercil End, where the land seems to have been part of the demesne. Grazing became increasingly important in the economy of Arden in the late Middle Ages for, in the aftermath of the Black Death, there was a change in land use, more being under pasture. In addition the animals could be easily managed by the reduced labour force.

Eastcote was a separate settlement and perhaps the site of the second Barston Domesday manor which also had a mill, then valued at 20d. This was possibly Caldeford Mill, which stood on the Blythe close to Eastcote Hall, the only known moated site in Barston.

Bickenhill was another open-field parish. The two Domesday manors of Church Bickenhill and Hill Bickenhill (the site now marked by Park Farm) had by the mid-13th century developed into three settlements, Middle Bickenhill growing up at the junction of Coventry Road and Middle Bickenhill Lane. Each had its own open-field unit and common meadows, with common grazing on the extensive Bickenhill Heath which lay to the north, now the site of the NEC.

Amid the open-fields there was little land available for independent farms but in 1240 Hugh de Arden was granted land called Hargrave 'to assart ... to enclose it and make ditches, and to take their profit of it as they please'; Hargrave Hall, now Hargrave Cottages, was the site of the house. Adjoining Hargrave was Castle Hill, part of Hampton manor although within Bickenhill parish, where Hugh de Arden had his second park. Dugdale thought the place was originally called *Bederichesley* and the site of a castle, possibly built by the Norman lords of Hampton during the turmoil of Stephen's reign and reduced by decree of Henry II. The site is now marked by mounds of earth, the remains of a moat and a 17th century house.

Also within Bickenhill parish lay the manor of Marston which, during the 12th century, was divided in two. The original manor at Marston Green became known as Marston Culy, the surname of the then lord. The moated manor house adjoined the open-fields and close by were the lord's park, St Leonards Chapel and Esthale Mill on Kingshurst Brook. There was only one assart, Old Moat Farm, at the edge of Marston Culy Green. The second manor, Wavers Marston, was held by the Wavers family. The settlement was probably in the area of Marston Hall, recently demolished for the extension of the airport, but a paucity of deeds makes its past difficult to determine.

The village of Lyndon lay at the junction of Wagon Lane, Barrows Lane and Old Coventry Road; first recorded in 1221 the name means 'at the lime tree'. Part of Bickenhill parish, although a detached portion, Lyndon had, by 1327, become a manor. Kineton manor, already in decline, adjoined Lyndon to the south and in time was absorbed by it. Thus Lyndon stretched from just east of Manor House Lane, where the manor house and chapel stood, to Kineton Green Road.

Adjoining Bickenhill is Elmdon, where the original settlement was probably based at Whar Hall, recently demolished. The earliest communal fields lay between the settlement and Elmdon Heath, and later a group was established athwart the Coventry Road. The manor house, rebuilt subsequently as Elmdon Hall, was close to the church, also rebuilt to enhance the park.

To the north of Bickenhill is Coleshill, given by Henry I to the de Clinton family. They granted land in Kingshurst and Alcott for the making of independent farms which, in time, became manors. Kingshurst, meaning 'the King's wooded hill', was held by the Montforts of Beaudesert who built a moated house, Kingshurst Hall. Although that is now demolished, the moat survives. Beside it is a mound with a wide ditch; of pre-13th century date it was raised higher and the ditch widened post-1290; it was possibly the site of a hunting lodge or look-out tower. Kingshurst Park, to the west of the Hall, was made in 1447; it still exists but as a wood known as Yorkswood, the York family being tenants of the Kingshurst Hall estate from 1767 to 1837. Babbs Mill, on the Cole south of Kingshurst, was also known as Kingshurst Mill although it was the manorial mill of Sheldon. Since the mill was founded, pre-13th century, the river has changed course and now follows the line of the mill-run.

Southeast of Kingshurst lay *Chelemundesheia*: Chelmsley Wood, meaning 'the enclosed woodland of Ceolmund', which was claimed by Margaret de Clinton in 1200 as part of her dowry together with 'all the wood called Witesmore'. The manor of Alcott or *Oldecoteshalle* adjoined Chelmsley Wood, Alcott Hall lying between Chelmsley and Alcott Woods and close to the extensive Coleshill Heath.

Adjoining Coleshill to the west is Castle Bromwich, originally known as Bromwich, meaning 'dairy farm in the broom', Castle being added during the 13th century. The Norman motte, built on an earlier defensive site, stood 25 feet above the bailey, was 25 feet across and would have been topped by a wooden stockade. The original settlement probably lay where Castle Bromwich

Hall now stands, the open-fields being adjacent. One field was close to the village and two others were on the opposite side of the Old Chester Road. Later the fields were extended and the village moved to its present site. When the present Castle Bromwich Hall was built c1599 the old manor house, close to the motte, was abandoned. A park at Castle Bromwich is recorded in 1291; later a moated house, Park Hall, was added. It was also known as Le Logge, suggesting that it was a hunting lodge. Owned from the 14th to the 17th century by the Arden family, Park Hall was described in 1414 as a manor.

It took about two centuries for the population to recover from the decimation caused by the plague and return to early 14th century size. For a century it did not rise at all, some survivors, it is thought, being so shocked and scarred by events that they shirked any responsibility, even marriage. Others delayed marrying and there was probably a drop in fertility.

For those without such fears it was a time of opportunity, many taking on the land of their dead neighbours to form larger and more profitable farms. In time they built new, stout, timber-framed houses, some of which still stand. Fewer people meant less demand for corn and much land fell out of arable cultivation. In Arden there was a move to the breeding of cattle and fattening them for meat, the animals doing well on the lush grass of the clay lands; there were also ample water meadows for hay. Some sheep were kept but generally conditions were probably too wet for large flocks. At Baddesley Clinton in the 1450s John Brome specialized in fattening cattle, buying about 70 animals a year which he sold after two years to butchers in Coventry and Warwick. Many smaller local men must have farmed on similar lines. It was probably the cows, oxen, steers and bulls of such small producers which were bought in the 1540s at Berkswell, and particularly at Hampton (possibly at the market as tolls were paid), by Thomas Hygginson on behalf of Peter Temple, a wealthy grazier. In 1547 he bought 135 animals at Hampton, paying about 15s for each cow. Later Hygginson with two others leased large areas of pasture in Berkswell for their own use.

In places piecemeal enclosure of the open-fields was slowly taking place. Enclosure enabled tenants to farm as they wished, free from the strictures of communal cultivation. Some grew flax and hemp, which gave rise to the small-scale but widespread craft industry of weaving. Linen, canvas, hurden and rope were produced, with by-products of linseed oil and animal food. The wool from the few sheep kept was prepared and spun at home, as were hemp and flax, then sent to a local weaver to make into cloth.

During the preparation of wool, hemp and flax the fibres were teased out with combs, the teeth being made of wire. The making of wire — wire-drawing — for the combs, and for pins, needles and fish-hooks was carried out in Solihull, part of the town's metal-making trade. This and two other trades, leather and clothmaking, were important to Solihull, the skinners, tanners, weavers, fullers, dyers and sheermen utilizing local hides and home-spun yarns.

The drop in the population affected the markets; Balsall, Meriden and Hampton had ceased by 1600, although several fairs continued. Even so a market grew up at Knowle, no doubt to take advantage of the many visitors to the Guild. The traders almost certainly set up their stalls at Golden End, the name implying a market, which probably ceased when the Guild was suppressed. Although Solihull market must also have suffered, it managed to survive, but subsequently neither town nor market expanded. Gradually, unable to compete with Birmingham, the market declined and by 1632 was 'little frequented'. During these years many Solihull craftsmen, incapable of supporting themselves, were helped by Whateley's Dole, a charity for 'decayed' tradesmen.

Those who survived best, tradesmen and farmers, had paying sidelines. The tradesmen had perhaps a cow and a pig, and the farmers a craft: smithing, making tiles, bricks, wooden tubs, pails, casks. If things went badly they gave support; if all went well the extra income paid for a better house with a brick and local stone chimney, tiled roof, more rooms and better furniture; from the 1560s such improvements became a general expectation. Many moated sites were abandoned and gradually new or rebuilt timber-framed houses dotted the Arden landscape.

Since the 15th century meat, particularly beef, had been the common food of the people but, as the population rose, and with it prices, meat could no longer be regularly afforded. In the 17th century bread and cheese became the staple diet, with pork and bacon occasionally. The Arden farmers began to move from beef to dairy production: butter and particularly cheese. In the 17th and 18th centuries Warwickshire cheese was famous, being produced in large amounts by local farmers, some having up to three cwt maturing in their cheese chambers. From c1610 more corn was grown, the surplus going to market as an increasing number of landless people looked for both food and work. Dairying and crop production were more labour intensive than pasturing and some found work in agriculture, others in crafts. Then these ceased to be side-lines and became full-time skilled trades.

Until mechanization killed them off, small-scale brick making, tanning, spinning, weaving, flax-growing and other necessary trades — carpentry, smithing, shoe-making, etc — played their part in the economy of the Arden villages as did malting, and wick-yarn making, a speciality of the Packwood, Hockley Heath, Monkspath area. Solihull became a small country town, a delightful backwater, enlivened only by the occasional fair.

ABOVE: Chester House, Knowle, now restored and used as the Library. Originally two mediaeval houses, it was joined into one c1600 by adding the central bay (behind the wheel). (SL) OPPOSITE ABOVE: Milverton House, Knowle, reputedly mediaeval but the timbering and chimneys suggest it is late 16th century. (JW) BELOW: Temple Balsall Hall. (SL)

LEFT: One of the oldest houses in Barston, its gable end facing the street. (JW) RIGHT: The courtyard of Temple Balsall. (WCRO) BELOW: The Saracens Head, Balsall Street, an ancient inn. (SL)

LEFT: Whar Hall, Elmdon, recently demolished. An 18th century house on an ancient site. (MF) RIGHT: Alcott Hall, an 18th century house on an ancient site, now Council offices. (JW) BELOW: Marston Hall, an early 16th century house recently demolished. (SL)

ABOVE: The Hall and Park at ELMDON c1860. CENTRE: Castle Bromwich Hall c1829. The ornate porch and third storey were added by Sir John Bridgeman c1660. (SL) BELOW: Chelmsley Wood. In spring it was full of bluebells. (JW)

From God and Goodness

The ancient churches of the Metropolitan Borough are built of local sandstone: a soft pink at Berkswell and Temple Balsall and a mixture of sober grey with warmer hues at Hampton, Solihull, Bickenhill, Meriden and Knowle. Excluding Temple Balsall and Knowle, all contain work of the 12th century, Berkswell, the least altered, having a Norman nave and chancel above a rare and remarkably fine crypt.

During the 13th, 14th and 15th centuries all the churches were partly rebuilt and extended, the size and style reflecting, as well as the glory of God, the economic status of the benefactor. Berkswell was made beautiful by the Mundeville family and the Earls of Warwick, Temple Balsall 'sumptuous and inventive' by the Knights Templar, and Knowle, 'a church of some ambition', was founded by Walter Cook.

No churches are mentioned in the Domesday Survey but the recorded presence of a priest at Ulverley and at Hampton suggests that at each a simple wooden one may have existed. Alternatively there may have been a field church — no building, but a place of prayer marked by a large wooden cross where people would gather and worship. Although neither church nor priest are recorded at Berkswell in 1086, there are indications that beneath the Norman crypt lie the remains of an earlier Saxon building. There are suggestions in legend and folklore that Berkswell was a place of pilgrimage, either to the Well, the waters reputedly having healing properties, or to the shrine of a saint. 'Saint' Milred, Bishop of Worcester, who died c774, is said to be buried at Berkswell but he appears not to be an acknowledged saint and it has been suggested that the shrine was to St Mildred, Abbess of Minster-in-Thanet who died in 725. She was buried in Canterbury but a relic of her might have been obtained by her kinsman, Ethelbald, King of the Mercians, and taken by him to Berkswell where he may have built a shrine.

Gradually parishes were established, their boundaries being defined, for the most part, by the 11th century. Bickenhill, a parish of about 4,000 acres, included Hill, Middle and Church Bickenhill as well as Wavers Marston, Marston Culy, Lyndon and Kineton. The last three each had their own chapel: Lyndon, in existence by 1329, was near Manor House Lane; the site of Kineton chapel was possibly Chapel Fields Farm, Lyndon Road, demolished in 1954, while that at Marston Culy, dedicated to St Leonard, was founded before 1347 but had ceased by the late 16th century, Chapel House Farm being built on the site. Later a new St Leonard's chapel was built elsewhere.

A parish of similar size was Meriden, the hilltop Church of St Laurence serving both parts of the village. The 15th century tower at one time had a stone spire which must have been visible for miles. Berkswell parish was larger, some 8,000 acres, and until 1894 included Barston (of about 2,000 acres). Barston had its own church, St Swithin, which was burnt down. It was rebuilt in red brick in 1721 on the old foundations. The plan is simple, and suggests that the original church was early mediaeval, perhaps Norman. Part of the original sandstone shell appears to be encased within the brick walls and there is old stonework in the tower.

Another 18th century church, with remnants of an earlier building within it, is St Mary and St Margaret, Castle Bromwich. When the Church was restored in 1891 it was discovered that the fine classical red brick exterior of 1726 enclosed a timber-framed building, timbers of great size, now encased in plaster, supporting an ancient roof. This core building was probably the chapel known to have existed in 1301, Castle Bromwich then being part of Aston parish.

St Nicholas, Elmdon is also an 18th century church, built in 1781 by Abraham Spooner to complement his newly built mansion, Elmdon Hall, which was adjacent. It replaced an earlier church on the site, which served the small parish of 1,000 acres.

When the town of Solihull was established a church dedicated to St Alphege — the Archbishop of Canterbury murdered by the Danes in 1012 — was founded. It grew large and grand under the patronage of the de Limesi and d'Oddingsells families and by the mid-14th century had almost reached its present size. To the south of the Church a spring occurred, referred to in mediaeval times as the Holy Well. Travellers may have broken their journey at Solihull to rest and pray by the Well and it may even have attracted pilgrims. The parish of Solihull was large and included Ulverley, Longdon, Shirley and Forshaw within its bounds.

Hampton was also a large parish, about 11,500 acres, Balsall, Knowle and Nuthurst being part of it until the 19th century. At Balsall the Knights Templar built their own chapel, a large building arranged in collegiate style. The chapel passed to the Knights Hospitaller with the rest of the Templar property but fell into decay after the order was suppressed in 1540. In 1662 the building was re-roofed and restored by Lady Katherine Levinson and her sister, Lady Anne Holbourne, and became the chapel to the nearby almshouses founded in 1671 by Lady Katherine. The chapel was again restored in 1849 by Sir George Gilbert Scott and became the parish church in 1863 when Balsall was separated from Hampton.

All the parishioners were supposed to attend Hampton Church but the distance for Nuthurst people was great and a chapel had been established there by the early 13th century. At Knowle the Arden family had their own chapel by 1225, but the village people were obliged to travel three miles and ford the Blythe to Hampton. Then in 1403 this became unnecessary when the present Knowle Church, founded by Walter Cook and dedicated to John the Baptist, St Anne and St Lawrence, was consecrated. Reputedly born in the village, Cook, having attained high office as a priest and grown rich, built the Church on land belonging to his parents. Consisting of a nave, north aisle, chancel and bellcote, it was soon extended when Cook and his father, Adam, founded a chantry to pray daily for the souls of the dead. A transept was built to house the chantry chapel where the masses were said, one and perhaps two priests officiating. The tower replacing the bellcote also dates from that time. Since 1921 part of the chantry chapel has been known as the Soldiers' Chapel and dedicated to the memory of those of Knowle who died in both wars.

In 1413 Cook founded the Guild of St Anne, a religious society similar to a modern benefit society, which ordinary men and women could join. The main object was to unite members in prayer and encourage them to observe holy festivals, but help was given to those in trouble. Each day the Guild chaplains celebrated masses for the good estate of living members and the souls of those who had died. The Guild was extremely popular with people from a wide area as the extant Register of 1451-1535 shows; during the period some 15,000 individuals joined. They were mostly substantial farmers and their families drawn from a 20 mile radius, but many lived elsewhere in Warwickshire and beyond. Some grander people — the Earl of Huntingdon, the Marquis of Dorset and their wives and numerous Abbots — also belonged. The 15th century Guild House was the headquarters where meetings and social events took place, and a hospice called The Cokke may also have been associated.

The Guild licence permitted five or six chantries, each with its own chaplain, who had no other task than saying daily mass. To keep the priests better occupied Cook, together with Lady Elizabeth Clinton, founded a College at Knowle in 1416. It was to consist of 10 chantries each with a priest, their purpose also being prayer; no doubt the same chaplains served both Guild and College. Controlled by an administrator, known as the Rector, the College was not a school but some teaching did occur, John Newborough, Master of Scholars, and his wife being granted a college house rent-free in 1425. To meet the needs of Guild and College the south aisle and nave clerestory were added to the Church c1420 and later the chancel was extended. The College buildings are thought to have stood east of the Church and abutted the chancel extension, preventing processions encircling the exterior of the Church. Thus a subway was built (now blocked up) beneath the sanctuary.

Perhaps the religious commitment so evident at Knowle was a thanksgiving that the devastating plagues of the previous century had ceased, and a plea that no further outbreaks would occur.

After Henry VIII's break with Rome, all ecclesiastical properties were valued and the small religious houses suppressed. In 1536 Henwood Priory was valued at £23 14s 3d per annum, there were six nuns plus the Prioress, Joan Higford, and seven dependants: a priest, a yeoman, two hinds and three dairy women. The house was described as 'ruynous and in moche decaye' but there were three bells worth 20s, 60 acres of wood, and stock and goods valued at £24 5s 1d. The Priory was surrendered with little protest, the Prioress receiving a pension of £3 6s 8d per annum. In 1540 the whole property was sold by the Crown to John Higford for £207 5s 0d. In the same year the Knights Hospitaller were obliged to surrender all their property to the Crown, including their church, land and buildings at Temple Balsall, which the King then gave to his new bride, Katherine Parr.

After the Dissolution of the abbeys and priories many chantries were voluntarily dissolved and their endowments used to found schools and almshouses. Those that remained were transferred to the Crown in 1545 and two years later all chantry properties, land, rents, jewels, monies were confiscated by the King's Commissioners. The College of Knowle and the Guild were suppressed, their lands and endowments confiscated, and the six resident priests given pensions. Because of its close association with the College and Guild the future of the Church hung in the balance; but it was retained due to the distance from Hampton Church and 'a great and daungerowse water wch ... so Rageth' that people were in 'daunger of peryshing'. Not until 1924 was the Blythe bridged at this point and even in the 1960s it was frequently impassable in winter.

There were chantry chapels in several local churches: at Hampton the late 15th century chapel is now used as the priest's vestry; at Berkswell, St Catherine's chantry was in the south aisle and there was possibly another chapel in the north aisle. A chantry for the soul of Sir John Wyard of Giants Den, Member of Parliament for Warwickshire and Mayor of London, was founded in the south aisle at Meriden in 1404. His fine alabaster effigy, of a knight in full armour, still remains. Another table tomb dated c1465 with the figure of a knight, possibly Sir John Walsh, lies in the north aisle, where a chantry for the souls of the family from Walsh Hall may have existed.

At Solihull a chantry for the souls of his parents was founded by Sir William d'Oddingsell in 1277 and the beautiful upper chapel of St Alphege purpose-built. The chantry priest lived and had his sacristy in the unusual crypt chapel beneath, where the fireplace which warmed him may still be seen. At the Reformation the endowments from this chantry, together with those of the chapels dedicated to St Catherine and St Mary, were allocated to pay the salary of a schoolmaster, leading in 1560 to the founding of Solihull Free Grammar School, now Solihull School.

The break with Rome made a great change in people's lives; there were fewer holy and fast days; the churches were plainer, wall paintings whitewashed over, the rood screens, the statues and candles removed; the services were conducted in English, with a new liturgy and no masses. The majority accepted the changes, were pleased when Queen Mary restored the old familiar ritual, but conformed again to the new services when Elizabeth ascended the throne. There were some, however, who remained faithful to Rome and who refused to attend the Church of England, as the law obliged them to do at least one Sunday per month or be fined one shilling per absence. These people became known as recusants and there were quite a number in Greater Solihull: at Balsall, Berkswell, Bickenhill, Hampton, Tanworth, Solihull, Knowle.

From 1580 Jesuit priests came secretly to England from Rome to provide services for the recusants. They travelled, usually by night, to isolated houses where small groups gathered to hear mass and occasionally to be baptised or married. If caught the priests were tried, invariably tortured, and executed. The penalties for recusancy increased from this time, many suffering great financial hardship, and even death, for their faith.

An official list of known Warwickshire recusants made in 1592 names two at Balsall, nine at Berkswell, one in Bickenhill, seven at Hampton, 20 at Packwood, 43 in Tanworth and 78 in Solihull and Knowle. Of the latter, 23 were wilful recusants, one William Huddesford 'had a child lately baptized by a popish prieste in secrett and refused to have it baptized at his parisshe churche'. Six others, five men and a woman, were committed to Warwick Gaol for obstinate recusancy in October 1592. They were poor and unable to pay for their own food in prison as required. They 'all agreed that they would not be persuaded to support the King of Spain or the Pope should they invade England and were allowed to go home upon bonds', a reminder that, despite the defeat of the Armada, invasion was still thought a possibility and that most Catholics were loyal Englishmen who simply wanted freedom of worship.

The high fines and imprisonments led many Catholics to reform, but in some cases this was a facade. Outwardly they conformed, attending church to prevent financial ruin, being married and having their children baptized in the parish church to ensure their legitimacy. However it is clear from a detailed study of contemporary records that the 1592 figures greatly underestimate how many wished to follow the old faith: in the period 1580-95 at least 27 at Berkswell, 15 at Bickenhill, 34 at Hampton and 104 at Solihull and Knowle.

There was a hope among Catholics that James I might have a more tolerant attitude towards religion, but this was not the case. Neither did he favour a more Puritan church, which others looked for. Desperation led to the Gunpowder Plot after which all but the most ardent of papists outwardly conformed for a time. There are references however to certain men and women who were so against the Church of England that they refused, even in death, any association. In 1612 John Field, a carpenter of Solihull was 'buried at night', Anne Greves in 1600 'was buried by women' and Margaret Huddisforde, the woman sent to prison in 1592, was in 1609 'buried by her sons', all presumably secretly and with the benefit of Catholic prayers in Latin.

As the century advanced, Catholics continued to be fined for non-attendance at divine service and some were 'excommunicated' by the Church of England, but their numbers did not diminish and were much the same in Berkswell, Bickenhill, Hampton, Solihull and Knowle in the 1630s and 1660s as they had been in 1580-95. At the same time, throughout Warwickshire, there was a growing band of low-church non-conformists: Dissenters. They and many others in the county supported the Parliamentary side in the Civil War. During the Commonwealth those clergy who would not follow the Puritan way were ejected from their livings and replaced by others. At Tanworth in 1646 Thomas Balgaye was removed and Ralph Hodges appointed in his place; likewise at Hampton Richard Pretty was ejected, Josiah Packwood taking his benefice. However, at the Restoration positions were reversed and Pretty, with many others, was rightly restored.

The ejected Puritan ministers continued to preach whenever they could, although they and their followers suffered much persecution, even more than the Catholics to whom Charles II was sympathetic. Illegal Baptist, Quaker, Congregational and Presbyterian conventicles were held at Coventry, Alcester, Warwick, Henley and Kenilworth and also in some villages. Meetings of Presbyterians were formed by 1669 at Coleshill, at Lapworth and at the house of Mr Willis in Hampton where 20 people frequently attended. At Knowle lived John St Nicholas, a minister ejected from Lutterworth in 1660. Here he sheltered other ejected ministers — John Gilpin, Mr Ede, James Wright — all of whom held conventicles. Wright, removed from Wootton Wawen, lived at Blue Lake House, Dorridge where he preached regularly to 'as many Hearers as two Rooms would hold' and also had a school. He was friendly with the vicar of Knowle, John Wilkinson, who had been removed from Ansley in 1660 but later conformed and acquired the Knowle living.

In 1672 freedom of worship for non-conformists was permitted and meeting houses were licensed, but in 1675 the licences were revoked and persecution began again; this finally ceased in 1689 under the Toleration Act. A licence was granted for Quakers to hold meetings at Fulford Heath, at the house of Francis Palmer where Friends had been gathering regularly since the 1660s, up to 120 attending. Small groups of Quakers also met at Meriden from c1673 to 1711. A meeting started at Berkswell c1689, prospered and grew, absorbing the Meriden group and another which met at Balsall Street. A meeting house was built in Berkswell, at the house of John Wheeler in 1750 where Friends met until 1783 when it closed; the property was sold in 1840.

The Presbyterians were licensed in 1689 to hold meetings in the barn of Ann Webb at Knowle, James Wright by then being too old to have them at his house. He died in 1691 and in 1695 Blue Lake House was again used for meetings, where they continued until 1722. Various houses in Berkswell were also used for meetings, Bradnocks Marsh being the chief venue from 1705.

For the Catholics there was some tolerance but they were still brought before the courts, the only respite being during James II's reign. The persecution was particularly bad from 1678-86 and 1691-3, when the fear of popish plots abounded. During those years the faith of the Catholics in Greater Solihull was supported by the Franciscans who, from the 1650s, had a mission centre at Baddesley Clinton. As their registers of 1657-95 show, travelling priests performed masses, baptisms and marriages over a wide area. In the 1680s there were at least 17 papists at Balsall, 24 at Berkswell, 20 at Bickenhill, nine at Hampton, 120 at Solihull and 17 at Knowle. After 1700 the Franciscan influence locally was reduced when their leader, Father Leo, died.

As the 18th century advanced people became less intense about religion; non-confomist chapels found their numbers dropping and by mid-century many small meetings had closed. There was less fear of Catholic plots and gradually the penal laws fell into abeyance.

About 1750 a small Catholic mission appears to have started at Solihull, probably at The Priory, a large Tudor house which stood opposite the west end of St Alphege Church. It was the home of Hugford Hassell who, in 1760 on land he owned at the edge of the town, built a priest's house with a small chapel hidden from the road behind it. Although illegal, no-one objected. The first priests to serve this chapel, dedicated to St Augustine, probably came from Baddesley Clinton but from 1775 there was a resident priest at Solihull caring for a wide area. After 1829 and Catholic Emancipation the congregation grew, the Hassall chapel being replaced in 1839 by a small, plain church designed by A.W.N. Pugin. It was extended in 1866, in 1878 when a new Presbytery was also built, in 1884, 1897 and 1904, much of the interior decorative work and some of the stained glass being designed and drawn by members of the artistic Pippet family who lived in the town.

By the late 18th century the low state of non-conformity in Greater Solihull was concerning ministers in Birmingham and Coventry. In 1797 a Baptist minister preached at Shirley, starting a chapel in Pear Tree Cottage, previously the Cock Inn, Olton Road where services were held for 48 years until a chapel could be afforded.

In the 1820s Mr John Sibree of Coventry made a survey of the county and found large areas lacking in spiritual enlightenment. He was particularly shocked by Solihull, the people being 'in almost total spiritual darkness' because the rector of St Alphege, jolly parson Curtis, was 'more addicted to the sports of the field than to the spiritual care of his flock'. Sibree tried to rent a cottage to start a small chapel but was refused as 'offence would be given to the rector'. Instead land was bought in Union Road and the Bethesda Meeting House opened in 1826. The first minister, William Hood, found the town 'a moral wilderness', the people prone to 'swearing, lying, drunkenness'. He was soon attracting 250 to his services and a prosperous Sunday School was founded. His missionary zeal also took him out into the villages to preach. A room was hired at Balsall Street, where for several years he held services for about 50 people and similarly at Shirley. Early in 1829 he opened 'a house for preaching at Monkspath Street' and in the same year he rented the schoolroom of a ladies' seminary at Knowle and gathered a large and attentive congregation. The £200 needed to buy a plot of land in Knowle High Street was given in 1834 and a chapel built. In 1834 Hood also opened preaching rooms at Salter Street, Catherine de Barnes, and Marston Green where a chapel was built in 1837.

For some years a group of non-conformists had met for worship at Millicent Cottage, Stratford Road, Hockley Heath. Through Hood's energies a chapel was built in Chapel Lane (Orchard Road) in 1837. At Hampton, Hood helped a small group to erect, in 1838, Providence Chapel on land given by the Simmonds family. By 1840 Hood's 'area' included 14 villages, 5,000 people, five chapels; at Solihull he had 40 chapel members, three lay preachers, 16 Sunday School teachers and 22 tract distributors. He resigned in 1848 and many meetings did not long survive the loss of his enthusiastic spirit. The Knowle chapel closed in 1855 but later re-opened and was kept going by visiting preachers. The Hockley Heath congregation declined rapidly after the Baptists built Christ Church in 1877 although it survived to the 1930s; the chapel at Hampton closed only in 1974.

The death of the Church of England rector, Charles Curtis, in 1829 brought the Reverend Archer Clive to Solihull. He re-pewed the church, put in a heating system, planted the lime trees which still edge the churchyard and built a large new Rectory, some panelling originally in Henwood Hall being installed. Almost immediately the people of Shirley asked for his help in acquiring a chapel-of-ease to save the long walk to St Alphege for services. This he gave and the chapel, dedicated to St James and built at a cost of £1,500 to seat 506, was opened in December 1831. The chapel was built the wrong way round with the altar at the west end, reputedly because of the noise from the Plume of Feathers where Birmingham 'sportsmen' had rowdy gatherings.

In 1843 Shirley was created a separate parish when Forshaw was added to Wythall. Knowle became an independent parish in 1858, Balsall in 1863, and Castle Bromwich as well as Nuthurst and Hockley Heath in 1878. Olton, growing rapidly as a residential area, was made a separate parish on the building of St Margaret's Church in 1881.

LEFT: Bickenhill Church c1860. RIGHT: Solihull Church, exterior and interior, c1860. The spire fell in high winds in 1757 causing considerable damage. The glass in the east window was given jointly by Thomas Chattock and Rev A. Clive.

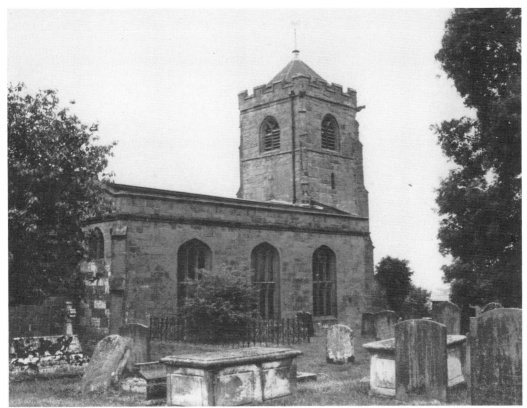

ABOVE: Meriden Church. (JW) BELOW: The ancient rectory at Solihull
demolished by Rector Clive c1831. (WCRO)

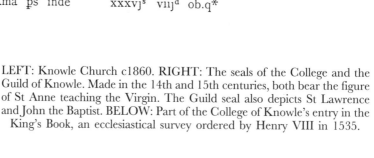

De quib₃

Resolucõ Redďus

Idm̃ computat in redďu resolut' aƀƀi monasterij
de Westm̃ ꝑ terr' iƀm ꝑ annū   xxxvˢ

Et allo^r eidm̃ ꝑ redďu resolut' priori Sc̃i Johĩs
Jerłm in Anglia ꝑ ann̄   vjˢ vjᵈ

Et allo^r eidm̃ ꝑ redďu resolut' priori ꞇ c̃onvent'
monasterij in civitate Coventr' ꝑ ann̄   vjᵈ

                              Sm̃ᵃ   xlijˢ

Elemosina

Et allo^r eidm̃ ꝑ quadm̃ elemosina dat' in die
anniv'sar' Walti Coke fundator' sui ut patet ꝑ
fundac̃oem ꞇ ordinac̃oem ejusdem Walti ꝑ ann̄
iijˢ ꞇ in die anniṽsar' Thome Kyxley nuꝑ
rector iƀm unĩs ƀñfactoꝤ ejusdm̃ capelle ꝑ ann̄
iiijˢ viijᵈ   in toto   vijˢ viijᵈ

                    Sm̃a   vijˢ viijᵈ
                    Sm̃a allocac'   xlixˢ viijᵈ
Et reman' clare ultra allocac' ꝑdict' ꝑ ann̄   xviijˡⁱ vˢ vjᵈ
              Xm̃a ꝑs indė   xxxvjˢ viijᵈ ob.q*

LEFT: Knowle Church c1860. RIGHT: The seals of the College and the
Guild of Knowle. Made in the 14th and 15th centuries, both bear the figure
of St Anne teaching the Virgin. The Guild seal also depicts St Lawrence
and John the Baptist. BELOW: Part of the College of Knowle's entry in the
King's Book, an ecclesiastical survey ordered by Henry VIII in 1535.

58

ABOVE: The Guildhouse, Knowle, c1905. On the facade is a sun-dial dated
1810. (SL) BELOW: Part of the Chantry Chapel, Knowle, known since 1921
as the Soldiers' Chapel. (SL)

59

ABOVE: Chapel Fields Farm, Olton, the site of the mediaeval Kineton chapel. It was demolished in 1954. (JW) BELOW: The classical 18th century exterior of Castle Bromwich Church. (SL) OPPOSITE ABOVE: The Catholic Church built by Pugin in 1839. The chancel, porch and Presbytery were added in 1878. (SL)

Hugford Hassall

LEFT: Blue Lake House, Dorridge in 1963, shortly before its demolition. Here Rev James Wright lived, preached and had his school. (JW) BELOW: The signature of Hugford Hassall who lived at The Priory and gave the land on which the first Catholic Church in Solihull was built. RIGHT: The Bethesda Chapel, Union Road, Solihull built in 1826, now the site of John Palmer Hall. (WCRO)

ABOVE: Knowle High Street; on the right, with the porch, the Non-Conformist Chapel built in 1837, now a dress shop. (IS) BELOW: Station Road, Marston Green c1905. The chapel in the distance was built by the Non-Conformists c1835. In 1863 it became the private chapel of the Digby family. Later, as St Leonard's, it was used by the C of E until a new church was built in 1938. (SL)

ABOVE: St James Church, Shirley. (JM) LEFT: The Dorridge Methodists in the 1960s at the opening of their first church, a 'terrapin', on the Bentley Farm site. (TG) RIGHT: The Wesleyan Methodist Chapel, Solihull, now used by the Local Authority. (SL)

ABOVE: Where Blossomfield Brook used to cross Church Hill, the brick bridge shows its position. The Rectory (right) had gardens stretching almost to the stream. (SL) BELOW: The 15th century pack-horse bridge at Hampton-in-Arden. (SL)

By Some Known Track

In the mediaeval period a network of lanes and tracks criss-crossed the area, leading from settlement to settlement and farm to farm. In addition there were several important highways: from London to Chester *via* Coventry and Meriden; from Birmingham to Stratford and to Coventry; from Dudley to Warwick *via* Birmingham, Tyseley and Church Hill, Solihull; Hillfield, Shelly, Monkspath and Hockley Heath. Yet the earliest ways, probably used since the Iron Age, were the saltways leading from Droitwich.

Using deeds and old maps T.F. Finnemore has found numerous 'salter lanes' and traced one route across Arden from Droitwich *via* Hanbury, Redditch, and Beoley to Salter Street, Tanworth, then along Creynolds Lane to Stratford Road. Three routes were then possible *via* Shelly or Hay Lane or Brick Kiln Lane, all arriving at Sulyhamford, where Blossomfield Brook crossed the foot of Church Hill, Solihull. Ascending the Hill, the saltway left Solihull and went through Hampton, passing west of the church if going north *via* Diddington to Chester, and *via* the pack-horse bridge and Berkswell if going to Coventry.

This salt route, apparently established before Solihull was founded, may have influenced the site of the town as two other roads are thought to have done: one the Dudley to Warwick road, and the second, a route similar to the saltway, from Worcester *via* Droitwich, Bromsgrove, Dickens Heath and Blossomfield Road (known in the 15th century as Wircester wey) to Solihull. Leaving the town *via* Hampton and Meriden, then on to Coventry, Leicester and Grantham, the road was used by monks, prelates and pilgrims travelling between the many religious houses. It was also frequented by merchants and traders transporting a vast range of goods, some of which were carried in and out of Wales and Bristol through Worcester. The Worcester-Grantham road was one of only three West Midlands roads shown on Gough's map of c1330, another being the Coventry-Chester road. Coventry was the major mediaeval trading centre of the Midlands to which merchants from all over England were drawn.

The road to Warwick was less important, for Warwick market was of only local interest but many people were obliged to visit the town, having business at the Castle or the court of Royal justice.

For all travellers the need was for a dry way, and many early roads carefully kept to the drift, avoiding the clay wherever possible. Crossing the numerous streams was a problem but good fords were looked for, and later, stout bridges. A bridge at Bradeford now called Stonebridge had been built by 1299, Monkspath Bridge by 1339 and Blythebrugge at Widney Manor by 1360.

The upkeep of all roads, both lanes and highways, was the responsibility of the parishes through which they passed. In theory, to keep them in repair under an Act of 1555, each householder gave four days' free labour or lent a team and cart; in fact, a Highway Rate was often levied and workmen hired. In both cases the maintenance usually consisted of filling the worst of the pot-holes with stones for there were no made surfaces. Parishes crossed by well-used roads found keeping them even barely passable a great burden. As wheeled traffic increased, post-1650, the problem grew and parishes were frequently fined at the Quarter Sessions for not repairing the worst areas. These were usually ill-drained places where, when ditches were blocked or heavy rain fell, the road was washed away or became a quagmire. Rudfin Lane (Kenilworth Road) Balsall Common, Rotten Row and Blue Lake in Knowle, Bradnocks Marsh and the road through Barston were particularly bad. Matters were not helped by those like Christopher West of Balsall who, in 1664, diverted a stream into the highway, William Daniell and his companions who, in 1667, dug three marlpits in the road near Stonebridge, and William Taylor of Hampton who ploughed up the lane to Bickenhill in 1660.

Bridges were a problem everywhere: Mouldings Bridge at Hampton (there by 1652), Blythe Bridge, Widney Manor, Sandals Lesser Bridge over Sandals Brook, and Easthall Bridge, Marston Green all needing repair at that time. The several bridges at Temple Balsall were kept up by the Earl of Leicester, who was thus excused any county taxes for bridge repair, but he was obliged to pay towards the rebuilding of Barford and Bidford Bridges, 'pulled down' in the Civil War.

In the late 17th century turnpike trusts began to be formed, the trustees undertaking to maintain a given section of road in return for tolls. One of the earliest portions of road in Warwickshire to be turnpiked was that from Dunchurch through Coventry to the bottom of Meriden Hill, in 1723. This was followed by the Birmingham-Warwick road *via* Knowle, and the Birmingham-Stratford road, both in 1725; the road from Lichfield to near Stonebridge *via* Coleshill, and from Birmingham to Stonebridge *via* Elmdon in 1744; and the connecting portion of the latter — Stonebridge to Meriden — in 1753. The roads from Birmingham to Castle Bromwich and from Chester to Stonebridge *via* Castle Bromwich were turnpiked in 1759 but the following year the chief landowners of Packington, which really meant Lord Aylesford, asked for the road to be diverted; for centuries it had passed through the park but this was no longer acceptable. The last local Trust was formed in 1772 when the road from Solihull to Balsall *via* Barston, and the Stonebridge-Kenilworth road were turnpiked.

Although toll roads invariably had poor surfaces and were often considered dangerous, the surveyors attempted to improve them through drainage, bridging and smoothing out difficult curves. The Warwick Road, at Olton, which originally curved along Old Warwick Road and Ulverley Crescent, was realigned along its present route, and in 1788 the Coventry Road was widened and its course from Hatchford Brook to Stonebridge moved slightly north. Even so the roads were still far from good, the Warwick and Stratford Roads being described in 1781 as 'much used and neglected'.

In 1784 the mail coach service was introduced to carry Post Office mail and parcels quickly and safely. An armed guard sat with the driver, only four passengers being carried. In order to adhere to the timetable, stops were short, all other traffic gave way, no tolls were paid, and turnpike gates were opened when the Mail's approach was announced by sounding a horn.

The London-Holyhead Mail passed through Stonebridge; and the London-Shrewsbury Mail travelled *via* Stratford and Birmingham, the latter route extended to Holyhead in 1808. A survey of both roads, with a view to improvement, was begun in 1810 by Thomas Telford who, like his contemporary, John Macadam, understood how to construct long-lasting roads. In 1811 it took 15½ hours to travel the 116½ miles from London to Birmingham *via* Stratford, the *Royal Mail* leaving at 8.00 pm and arriving at 11.30 am, an average of seven and a half miles per hour. On a Macadam road it was possible to average 10 miles per hour. Telford renovated the whole Holyhead road, the final route being *via* Coventry, Meriden, Stonebridge, Birmingham and Shrewsbury. Meriden Hill was lowered at a cost of £5,500 and the section to Pickford Brook improved.

There were many inns along the turnpikes, mostly in villages and towns. Not all were welcoming, as Lady Luxborough of Ullenhall discovered when she arrived at the Saracen's Head, Shirley, late one night in 1747. Despite much knocking she was ignored, 'we saw a good fire in the kitchen' but the 'maid who was sitting by it, took her candle and went to bed'. It was necessary to change horses about every eight miles and some roadside inns, the White Lion at Hockley Heath, the Black

Boy, Knowle; Bedlams Inne, Chadwick End, and George-in-the-Tree, Balsall are shown on 18th century maps. At Meriden the chief inn was the Bulls Head described as 'the handsomist inn in England'. Yet the Hon John Byng in 1789 found it 'deficient in every comfort' and 'only fit for waggoners'. Even so Queen, then Princess, Victoria stayed there in 1832.

The peak of the coaching era was the early 1830s when 10 coaches went daily to London *via* Shirley, and four *via* Solihull, the latter calling at the Barley Mow and occasionally the George. This success was brought to a sudden end by the coming of the railway, the opening of the London to Birmingham line in 1838 reducing the coaches from 22 to four a day. Away from the railway routes coaches continued longer, but many roads were disturnpiked by the 1870s.

Contemporary with the growth of coach travel was the era of canal mania. A network of canals was cut around Birmingham, enabling its products to reach a wide area. A canal linking Stratford with Birmingham and the Black Country was proposed, and in 1793 authorized. A survey, made by John Snape, suggested a route which branched off the Worcester-Birmingham canal at King's Norton, then went *via* Solihull Lodge, Dickens Heath and Illshaw Heath to Hockley Heath, continuing to Stratford *via* Lapworth, Lowsonford, Wootton Wawen and Wilmcote. Capital of £120,000 was raised, mostly from local men, and work began, directed by Josiah Clowes.

The Birmingham Canal Company, which monopolized the Birmingham canal system and bought up any company with schemes rivalling its own, was furious at the Stratford Canal being permitted and immediately promoted the Birmingham-Warwick canal, also authorized in 1793. Capital of £130,000 was raised, with a further £50,000 in 1796. The work went ahead well and the 22½ miles were completed in 1799. The route was *via* Small Heath, Olton, Catherine de Barnes and Henwood to Knowle, where a flight of six locks lowers the canal 42 feet; then *via* Chessetts Wood, Kingswood, Rowington, Shrewley and Hatton to Warwick. The canal was fed by streams along the way and also by Olton Reservoir, constructed at the same time by flooding a valley through which ran Folly (*alias* Hatchford) Brook. Reputedly Napoleonic prisoners-of-war did the work, but this is not certain.

The Stratford Canal meanwhile, having reached Hockley Heath by 1796, ran out of money. Work started again in 1799 but it was 1802 before the stretch to Kingswood was completed. Not until 1812 was the southern section started, Stratford being reached in 1816.

Both canals made the transportation of heavy goods — coal, bricks, flour, grain, stone, lime — easier and thus cheaper and more readily available. As a result the price of coal fell and cheap machine-made bricks eventually killed the local trade. The goods were off-loaded at small wharves along the routes; lime dug and burnt at Copt Heath and other local lime-kilns, grain, and possibly flour, from nearby wind and water mills — Olton, Copt Heath, Henwood, Solihull Lodge — being on-loaded.

The canal made no major impact on Solihull for industry did not settle along its bank until the late 19th century, when Solihull Gas Works was built. The railway by contrast brought waves of people in its tow.

The first railway line across Greater Solihull was opened in 1838 by the London and Birmingham Railway. There was a station at Hampton, in Old Station Road, but not at Berkswell until 1852, or at Marston Green until after 1860, for originally only long-distance, not local traffic was considered important. At first travelling by train was neither comfortable nor cheap, but gentlemen from a wide area, keen to reach London in five and half hours, entrained at Hampton. A single first-class ticket cost £1 12s 6d; horses (50s each), carriages (75s or 55s depending on size) and grooms could also be taken and many people did this. Until 1842 the railway route from Birmingham to Derby was also *via* Hampton, then a new line from Lawley Street to Whitacre made this unnecessary. It went *via* Castle Bromwich, where a station was opened.

Gradually the railway spread its tentacles and in October 1852 the Great Western Railway opened the line from Birmingham Snow Hill to Oxford and thus to Paddington with stations at Solihull and Knowle, the journey taking less than three hours. Although called Knowle, the station was at Dorridge, then a place with few inhabitants. It is said that the railway company was unable to obtain land for the line, unless they agreed to the station and to certain express trains stopping there. Mr Muntz of Umberslade, who made this bargain, built the Forest Hotel so that he might stay the night there prior to travelling to London. The station approach remained a private road until recent years and to preserve this status was closed for one day each year. Dorridge rapidly developed as a middle-class residential area, the first roads being close to the station.

Berkswell Station (then called Dockers Lane) opened in 1852. Down the line at Hampton a new station was built, on the present site, in 1868 by the London and North Western Railway. For the convenience of Sir Frederick Peel of Hampton Manor, a Railway Commissioner, express trains stopped regularly and continued to do so until the opening of Birmingham International. By the 1860s the Hampton-Whiteacre line was reduced to single track and closed completely in 1917.

The opening of a station at Olton in 1869 led to another middle-class commuter village growing up. Local services became increasingly important: a station was opened at Widney Manor in 1899, new lines from Berkswell to Kenilworth in 1884, and from Birmingham to Henley in 1908 with stations at Shirley, Wood End and Danzey Green.

Initially there was much opposition to the railways, especially from landowners, and some routes were changed. Lord Aylesford had the Hampton line moved so as not to touch Packington Park, but the embankment, a mile and a half long and 35 feet high, which stopped the wind reaching Bradnocks Marsh windmill, was not demolished, despite the owner winning his case against the railway.

From 1853 it was also possible to travel by horse omnibus from Birmingham, *via* Shirley, to Henley and Stratford, none of which had stations. By 1863 Shirley had a daily service leaving the Saracen's Head at 8.30 am and returning from Bull Street at 6.00 pm. In 1879 there were six 'buses daily each way, and by 1900 'buses ran every two hours, the fare 6d. The 'bus conductor offered a special service: fetching tripe from a stall in the Bull Ring, money and cans were picked up at the Saracen's Head and the filled cans returned on the next 'bus. The first motor 'buses ran in 1912 and by 1914 a service *via* Shirley was operating regularly between Birmingham and Stratford.

68   OWEN'S NEW LIST   Weſtm.

Solyhull (107). May 10, Oct. 10, cattle, ſheep, and horſes. April 29, Oct. 12, cheeſe, hops, and cattle.

Southam (83). Eaſter-Monday, Monday after Holy-Thurſ. July 10, horſes, cows, and ſheep. *M.*

Stratford upon *Avon* (94). Thurſday after Lady-day, May 14, Sept. 25, Thurſday ſe'nnight after Sept. 25, for cloth, cheeſe, feed, wheat, hops, and all ſorts of cattle. The day after the laſt is a ſtatute for hiring ſervants. *Th.*

Sutton (106). Trin-Mond. Nov. 8, ſheep and cattle. *M.*

Tamworth (107). April 12, for cattle. Sept. 12, for cattle and cheeſe. *S.*

WARWICK ** (93). May 12, July 5, horſes, cows, and ſheep. Sept. 4, ditto, and cheeſe. Nov. 8, horſes, cows, and ſheep. *S.*

The dates of Warwickshire Fairs; the type of information provided by guides for coach travellers.

ABOVE: Balsall Street, typical of the width of many 19th century main roads.
(SL) BELOW: The George-in-the-Tree Inn, Balsall Common, late 19th
century. (SL)

OPPOSITE ABOVE: The Bulls Head, Meriden, 1752, not to be confused with the present Bulls Head. The inn closed c1850 and became a house, Darlaston Hall, demolished in the 1960s. Flats now occupy the site opposite the pool. LEFT: The Bradford Arms, Castle Bromwich, a coaching inn on the Chester Road, built in 1723, probably acquired this name in 1819, having previously been the White Lion. (JW) RIGHT: 15-17 Chester Road, Castle Bromwich, once a coaching inn, the Bridgeman Arms. When Orlando Bridgeman became Earl of Bradford in 1815 the name changed to the Bradford Arms. The inn closed in 1819 and the name was transferred. (SL) BELOW: The Barley Mow, Solihull, pre-1900 before it was partially rebuilt. A busy coaching inn, it was previously known as the Limerick Arms. (SL) ABOVE LEFT: A canal-side inn; the Anchor, Wharf Lane, Solihull. (WCRO) RIGHT: The iron milestone which stood against the wall of Bradford House, Warwick Road, Solihull. (WCRO) BELOW: The Drawbridge Stores and Beerhouse, Shirley, on the Stratford-upon-Avon canal, where boatmen could buy food and boat-chandlery and have a convivial drink. (JM)

ABOVE: The station approach and Forest Hotel, Dorridge. (SL) BELOW:
Marston Green Station post-electrification. Since this photograph was taken,
the level crossing has been closed and the station rebuilt. (SL)

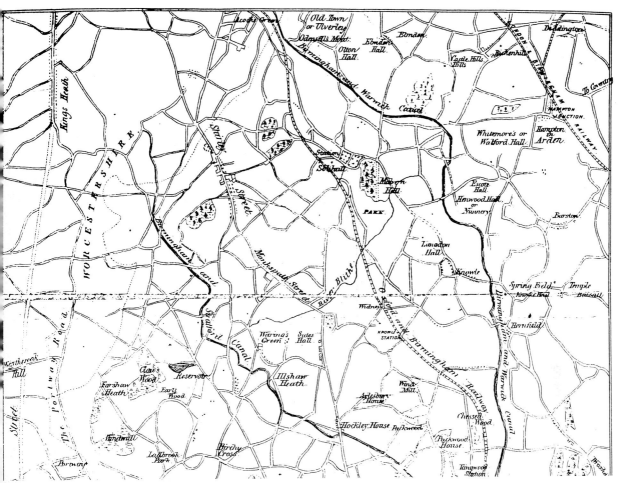

ABOVE: A map of c1860 showing the canals, railway lines and stations.
BELOW: The horse-bus to Birmingham waits outside the Saracens Head,
Shirley c1913. Just beyond the lamp-post (left) stood the turnpike tollgate
which blocked the road. (SL)

73

ABOVE: Olton Windmill 1897, built c1830-40, stood between Lode Lane and the canal and near Solihull Wharf and was demolished c1900. (JW)
BELOW: Dr Bernays, a Solihull GP, was an enthusiastic early motorist who owned several vehicles; here he is at the wheel in 1903 with Fripp, his chauffeur. (SL)

Improve my Youthful Mind

In the Middle Ages education was provided by grammar schools, usually situated in towns, where the boys (there were no girl pupils) were taught Latin and English grammar but little else. Such a school is reputed to have existed in Solihull from the time of Richard II but there is no firm supporting evidence. The earliest known local place of learning was that established by the College of Knowle in the 15th century. Lessons may have been held at the master's house which was probably close to the Church. When the College was dissolved the school was presumably closed and no more is heard of it.

When in 1547 the chantries were suppressed, the colourful decoration and rich ornaments in the chapels stripped off, and the endowments confiscated by the Crown, some parishes managed to retain part, if not all, their chantry land to found a school or almshouse. At Solihull the income of the land, which had previously supported the chantry chapels of St Catherine and St Mary, was allocated in 1560 to pay the salary of a schoolmaster, and this is the acknowledged date of the foundation of the Free Grammar School, now Solihull School.

Edward Pole, the first master, was paid £8 per year and after 1566, when the revenue of St Alphege's chantry was also assigned to the school, £12 per year. The schoolhouse was near the Church in Park Road; it still exists and, much altered, is known as Malvern House. Here Pole and his successors taught English, Latin and Greek, free, to the sons of all Solihull parishioners who wished them to be educated. At 14-plus the boys might go to Oxford or Cambridge and then into the professions; thus a clever but poor boy was able to improve his position in life. A Lower or English School for younger boys and those with less ambition was started in 1574; the lessons were in English only and taught by a second master or usher. The Lower School was always well patronized, for most Solihull parents simply wanted their sons to learn arithmetic and to read and write.

In 1592 John Horne was appointed master of the Upper School, his salary, £12 per annum, remaining the same throughout his 40 years in the post. During his time much building took place at the schoolhouse which was also the Horne's family home. When he died in 1635 the house consisted of four bedrooms upstairs and a hall, parlour, buttery and schoolroom downstairs, the lessons for both Upper and Lower schools held in one room. Horne almost certainly took boarding pupils to supplement his income: boys from outside Solihull parish whose parents paid him tuition fees as well as for their food and lodging.

A school similar to Solihull Lower, with the majority of the lessons in English but with some Latin instruction, existed at Berkswell at that time. It was greatly valued by local people and supported by charity funds. By the mid-16th century most parishes had quite a sizeable 'charity estate', consisting of houses and pieces of land bequeathed over the centuries by parishioners for the benefit of the Church, the poor, the roads etc., and which was usually administered by trustees known as feoffees. Berkswell parish was no exception and had a charity estate of some value, but in the 1580s the Marrow family, the lords of the manor, claimed the various charity lands as their own and started law suits to obtain them. The parishioners, led by Oliver Matthew of Mercote Hall and Eleanor Wilmore, refuted the claim, which went to the Court of Chancery. Finally in 1592 the property was confirmed as belonging to the parish, for the 'public good use' of Berkswell people and not the Marrows.

The school was first referred to in 1589, during the court proceedings, but is thought to have existed before that. By the early 17th century the building was in need of some repair: 1,000 tiles were purchased for the roof, a new brick hearth laid and a new lock put on the door. Thought to have been close to the Church, it may have occupied the site of the present school, rebuilt in 1839.

John Lavender of Berkswell, schoolmaster, who died in 1583, almost certainly taught at the parish school but may have also taken private boarding pupils. He appears to have been a gentleman; his widow Dorothy, *née* Wilmore, came from a landed family and at her death in 1602 was one of the wealthiest people in the parish. She was possibly a kinswoman of Eleanor Wilmore. The Lavenders also farmed and lived in a large house, probably Lavender Hall.

Edward Cheesenbury, a Mr Tussor (at a salary of £4 per year), Mr Davis and William Bott were in turn masters at Berkswell between 1603 and c1650. Bott, who like Cheesenbury was proficient in Latin, was only 18 years old when he taught at the school and had not yet received his degree at Cambridge. He may have been the son of Laurence Bott, the rector of Berkswell during the Commonwealth. The social standing of schoolmasters at that time was not high and many young men with degrees taught while awaiting higher preferment, or combined it with another job, frequently that of curate. Thomas Man, schoolmaster at Berkswell for 34 years in the late 17th century, was also a curate at Elmdon. He had no degree, was described as 'a very illiterate but pleasing man', yet taught Latin grammar. In 1691 he was appointed rector of Elmdon, where he died in 1719.

The idea of teaching ordinary village children to read and write gained ground as the 17th century progressed. The non-conformists were particularly keen and, after the Restoration, many dispossessed Puritan clergy earned a living by opening small schools. Other schools were founded by wealthy patrons, although most were obliged to charge a small fee unless there was a special endowment for poor children. At Packwood Miss Frances Fetherston by a will of c1660 wished to found a school. She left the interest on £400 to buy ground, build a schoolhouse and pay a master £20 per year salary. Whether the school was established is not clear and there is no further record of it.

More successful was Lady Katherine Levison's school at Temple Balsall, founded in 1671. The grand-daughter of Robert Dudley, Earl of Leicester, Lady Katherine, by will, left her estate at Balsall to found an almshouse or hospital for 20 poor women. A chaplain was to read them prayers twice daily and, for his salary of £20 per annum, also to teach, free, 20 of the poorest boys in the parish until they were fit to be apprenticed. The school flourished and still survives, as does Hampton-in-Arden village school, endowed by the will of George Fentham, a local boy made good.

Born in 1630, apprenticed in Birmingham probably as a mercer, Fentham was successful, leaving a large estate at his death in 1698. His sister, Dorcas, married the son of the Puritan vicar of Hampton and their son, Samuel Packwood, had a school in Hampton in the late 1680s. Samuel was following in his grandfather's footsteps, for Josiah Packwood taught at Nuneaton Grammar School until 1647, when he was given the Hampton living. Fentham, wishing to ensure that all Hampton boys attended school and then learned a trade, left £20 per year to pay a schoolmaster's salary and £5 for apprenticeships. Unfortunately his trustees were lax and it was 40 years before his will was executed, but in 1738 there was again a school in Hampton. Fentham also left money for teaching poor Birmingham boys and in 1949 these funds supported eight children at the Blue Coat School.

At Knowle a school appears to have existed c1605 but at the time they were often short-lived, sometimes through lack of support or simply because the teacher moved on. Later, in the 1660s James Wright, ejected from his benefice, taught at his home, Blue Lake House, Dorridge. He had mostly boarding pupils as Dorridge was then quite isolated. By the 1680s there was again a school in Knowle village, John Simmonds being the master. He and his wife, Susanna, had nine children, the first four dying while small and within an 18 month period. Greatly respected, Simmond was a churchwarden in 1688, 1689 and 1703. He was followed by Ebenezer Smith, and in 1721 by Thomas Treherne. By that date provision had been made by the Greville family, lords of the manor, for an equal number of poor boys and girls to be taught at the school, free. By the Hon Sarah Greville's charity twelve children also received an annual gift of clothes: a blue coat, orange breeches and waistcoat, plus a shirt, stockings and shoes for each boy; a gown and petticoat of blue stuff bound with orange, plus a bonnet, shift, apron, tippet, shoes and stockings for each girl.

Treherne, followed by his son, also Thomas, kept school at Knowle until 1800, their pupils being a mixture of those taught free, fee-paying day children and some boarders. The small, free, pupils were taught to read by assistants, both men and women, none of whom stayed long. One of the boarders was Walter Savage Landor. The son of a Warwick doctor, he was sent to school at Knowle aged four and a half, and remained five years, going on to Rugby in 1783. Landor was a brilliant scholar; he remembered Treherne fondly, and his happy days at Knowle.

Dame schools, where for a few pence children could learn their letters often from a semi-literate widow, had existed in many places for a long time and continued to do so, but numerous charitable bequests enabled an increasing number of children, particularly girls and the poor, to learn more. In the late 17th and early 18th centuries village schools were started at Elmdon, during the rectorship of Thomas Man, at Coleshill, Castle Bromwich, and Tanworth. Coleshill already had a grammar school founded in 1520, but William, Lord Digby, seeing the need for a school where girls could be taught useful skills — to read, sew, knit, spin — and boys to write and cast accounts 'to qualify them for being bailiffs and gentlemen's servants', used money left by his brother, Simon, for this purpose. Other bequests provided apprenticeships and in 1708 Lord Digby gave a house for a girls' school. Later in 1730, concerned about the poor children of Marston Culy, he ensured that 10 of them might attend Sheldon Charity School.

At Castle Bromwich a school was endowed in 1661 and was still open in the 1690s. William Sadler, possibly the schoolmaster, took over the endowment and, by his will of 1703, left his cottage for use as a Free School and master's house, 10 poor boys or if sufficient could not be found, 10 poor girls being taught. Later the Bridgeman family left sums to teach 16 additional boys and girls and to set some of them apprentice. A school may have existed at Tanworth before 1739 but it was not free. In that year it was decided that all children worthy of charity, including those in the Workhouse, should be taught by Thomas Woollaston to read and say their catechism. The parish being so widespread, a second school was opened at Salter Street in 1819, both being supported by the charity estate income.

At Solihull there was no school for poor girls until Martha Palmer left £50 by her will of 1723. The interest accumulated until 1743 when a house and three acres of land were bought for £70, and lessons begun. Two years later Elizabeth Fisher, a kinswoman of Martha, left £60 to support the endowment. Limited to 15 girls, a new school was built for them, plus infants, in Mill Lane in 1812. It moved again in 1830 to School Lane, giving it its name. Poor girls at Meriden were taught to read from 1749 by the bequest of 16s a year from Rights Charity but Meriden boys had to wait until 1781 to attend school, the master's salary of £20 being provided by the will of Henry Barnett. At Bickenhill there is no mention of a school until 1797 but it is thought that one must have existed previously, as so many people were able to sign their names when they married.

Thus by c1750 most of the villages of Greater Solihull had a school, invariably held in a house or cottage where the master also lived. The children, of varying ages, were usually taught together in one room, often in crowded and somewhat chaotic conditions. Most children learned to read if they attended regularly and for long enough, but many parents thought school a waste of time. Boys over six years could find work and contribute much-needed small sums to the family income, and at 10 years could earn approximately a fifth of a man's wage. Girls under 10 were not employable but at school they were not always taught writing and arithmetic, instruction in sewing and spinning being thought more important. How well those who attended learned depended on the master who was often, by then, a man who had failed in other fields. The children were expected to emerge obedient and grateful to their betters and, ideally, able to read the Bible; the boys able to write and add up. Using their ability to sign the marriage register (as against making a mark) as a test, the men and women of six local parishes, marrying between 1754 and 1773, showed a fair degree of application and competence. At Knowle 76% of the men could sign and 55% of the women; at both Meriden and Hampton 62% of the men could write their names despite Meriden apparently not having a school. The village, however, was open to the influence of many travellers and it may have been expedient for those serving them to be able to write. At Balsall 59% of men could sign and 56% at Elmdon and Berkswell. Only at Elmdon were the women more able than the men, 58% signing the register. Of the Meriden women 49% could sign but only 32% of those at Hampton and 30% at Berkswell and Balsall.

A good teacher might encourage a really bright boy and, with the patronage of the parson or squire, help him to widen his horizons. The best the rest could hope for was an apprenticeship in a trade which offered more opportunity than being a farm labourer. Boys were set apprentice to a variety of trades, chiefly blacksmith, tailor, baker, shoemaker, weaver or carpenter, in their own or neighbouring parishes, but as Birmingham and the Black Country became more industrialized, children were also apprenticed there. Many parishes had a policy of sending children out of their home parish so that they were no longer its responsibility if they fell on hard times. Solihull and Knowle were particularly adept at apprenticing in Birmingham and in specialized trades. By 1703 Thos Warrell, tailor of Deritend, had three apprentices from Knowle, and Luke Dolphin, sword cutler of Yardley, took on his second Knowle boy in 1720. Others from both parishes went to Walsall, Bilston and Birmingham between 1720 and 1830 to learn how to make, among other things, buttons, buckles, toys (small items), guns, spurs, snaffles, thongs, wire, perukes and wigs. Girls were occasionally apprenticed, usually in spinning, sewing or housewifery, but Solihull sent Sarah Wilson to be a spur-maker, Elizabeth Grosvenor a nailer and Mary Sherwin a Coventry ribbon weaver, Knowle sending Elizabeth Aylesbury to be a snuff-maker in Walsall and Mary Dike a mantua maker.

In the late 18th century, life in England began to change. There was a dramatic increase in the population: more children, more poor people. The growth of industry and war with France brought prosperity to manufacturers and large farmers. They wished their sons to be educated, not only in classics but in subjects useful for business: geography, science, advanced maths, history. Schools such as Solihull Grammar — which had enjoyed a golden period of classical scholarship when John Crompton was head (1704-34), his pupils including the Greek scholar John Taylor and poets Richard Jago and William Shenstone — offered none of these subjects, the syllabus being much the same as in 1560. As a result private schools, where middle-class boys could receive a practical all-round education, came into being. It was probably in the 1780s that John Powell opened such a school at Solihull. He was already teaching at the Grammer School, in charge of the Lower School. Somehow he managed to satisfactorily combine the two posts and continued to do so until his death in 1803. He left his own school to his nephew, John Powell junior, who also took over his uncle's position at the Grammar School; he remained as usher until 1812, when he resigned.

Powell's School prospered, having up to 150 pupils, many of them boarders. Irving Van Wart, a nephew of the American writer Washington Irving, was a pupil c1820 and in later years recalled his happy days in Solihull. During his time the School was in The Priory, but this house was occupied by the Hassall family until after 1803 and could not have been its original home. A lease of 1804 reveals that Powell then taught school at a house in High Street, almost certainly the Manor House. The schoolroom was to be enlarged, along prescribed lines, at his expense, suggesting that the number of pupils was rapidly growing. Later Powell moved to The Priory which he bought and extended, and where the boys had a large garden and field in which to play and fly their kites. He died there in 1838 having taken arsenic, in despair over the misconduct and extravagance of his own two sons.

Some middle-class daughters were also sent to school and given a genteel education, including music, drawing and dancing, in the hope that they would make a good marriage. In 1806 Miss Griffen kept a girls' boarding school at Linden House, next door to the George and now part of the hotel. Later it was taken over by Mrs Wimbridge and her daughter Caroline, who Van Wart recalled 'at stated hours on every fair day' took their charges for a walk, 'their graceful forms and bright faces ... marshalled two and two'. He also remembered partnering girls from this school and another in the town, probably Miss Wakefield's, during dancing lessons held at the Town Hall which then stood in The Square. The couples, paired by the master, were not allowed to speak; Van Wart longed to dance with Amanda Bushel but was allotted 'a dimpled beauty' and could only 'enjoy the thrilling pressure' of Amanda's fingers when they met 'in the mazes of the dance'. It was all very innocent and, during six months' mute adoration, her only response was a blush and 'sparking of the eye'.

Linden House, under various owners, remained a school for most of the century. It was the largest and best of several in the town for, as the atmosphere of Birmingham and the Black Country grew dirtier, better-off parents increasingly sent their children to board at the numerous small schools in Solihull and the surrounding area. These included Richard Thompson's Academy for boys at Bradford House, Solihull, John Blewitt's 'classical and commercial' boarding school at Castle Bromwich, Captain Hill's at Meriden, Rev Charles Bickmore's 'establishment for sons of the nobility and gentry' which opened at Berkswell Hall in 1844, and Lady Byron's Agricultural School at Copt Heath Farm. Opened in 1842, this boarding school offered a different kind of education: for six guineas a quarter, boys of 12-plus, often the sons of farmers, were taught land surveying as well as the usual subjects. Younger boys were also taken and there was another section for skilled farm labourers at Bentley Heath. Lady Byron, who had advanced ideas, inherited the Longdon Hall estate from her family, the Millbanke Noels.

As the number of children increased, larger village schoolrooms were needed. At Hampton the Fentham Trust built a new boys' school, with master's house attached, in 1782. It cost £152 3s 8½d and still stands in Fentham Road; in later years it proved too small and larger premises were built adjacent. Generous benefactors gave land, and local farmers subscribed to new purpose-built schools: for girls at Meriden on the 'old Bowling Green' in 1813 and for boys elsewhere in the village in 1823; at Shirley in 1836, at Hockley Heath in 1837, at Forshaw in 1847 and also at Bickenhill, the gift of the Earl of Aylesford; for girls at Hampton in 1849. Barston had its first recorded school in 1847, Packwood by 1845, with a new building in 1862. On average these schools could take about 50 pupils and several had a teacher's house attached.

Such concern for the young was not altogether altruistic; throughout the 19th century there was a fear of social unrest, and many thought some learning, together with the discipline and religious teaching instilled at school, might control it. Others, including educationalist Andrew Bell, feared that 'elevating ... the minds' of the labouring poor 'above their condition' might make them 'discontented and unhappy in their lot'.

It was Bell who c1803 devised the monitorial or National system which enabled one person to teach numerous children. The master taught simple lessons to some of the older pupils who were appointed monitors. Each monitor then passed the lessons on to a group of about 10 children. The subject matter was elementary, learned by rote, then chanted repeatedly. The system required strict discipline, allowed no questions or opinions, forcing facts into young minds, yet it worked, up to a point, and was cheap.

By 1850 most of the local schools operated the National system including Solihull Lower, which in that year broke away from the Grammar School and moved into a new building in Park Road, on the site of the present St Alphege Infants. It succeeded quickly; in 1847 the pupils were reported to be 'intelligent and well taught' by Mr Bond the master, who also gave them music lessons. A separate department was built for girls and infants in 1862 at a cost of £415, the Palmer Charity girls moving there, the Workhouse children also attending. Education was not yet free and most church schools charged 2d per week per child, to which many parents objected.

A log-book of the 1860s for Park Road Girls' reveals that E. Harris was kept at school by Mrs Beard of Hillfield Hall and when she ceased to pay, Harris had to leave. It also records that parents kept their girls away at hay and harvest time, for gleaning, and at various times for picking cowslips, acorns, potatoes, fruit. Not surprisingly many pupils failed their arithmetic and writing tests.

Some children walked quite a distance to school and, if the weather was bad, they stayed at home. In January 1865 attendance was affected for almost three weeks by snow-blocked lanes. A shoe-club ensured that the children were well shod, but in 1866 the new shoes ordered were 'not ready' and many were absent, their old ones being 'too thin'. There were frequent outbreaks of measles, whooping cough and smallpox, which spread rapidly through the school and town. Most girls left school to go into service, the greatest excitement in their young lives perhaps being a visit to the Diorama Show at the Town Hall or to the wild beast show to which Miss Chattock of Silhill House treated them in September 1869. The Park Road schools prospered; the buildings were extended in 1872, but in 1880 were bursting at the seams, school attendance being compulsory for all children up to the age of 10, although not yet free.

The Grammar School meanwhile made a new beginning. Its record had been poor for many years, with few pupils and a lazy master; c1840 a new head was appointed and a more practical syllabus introduced, but with little effect. In 1850 the head changed again and it was decided to make the school fee-paying; after 300 years the Grammar School was no longer free; it cost £2 per annum. The fees were gradually increased and, from 1860, under the headship of Rev James Bennett, the school greatly improved and the curriculum was widened. A new system of management by a Board of Governors was instituted in 1879; they quickly realised that, although the buildings had recently been extended and modernized, this was not enough. A site was acquired and in 1882 the school moved to Warwick Road, since when it has grown in numbers and reputation.

Berkswell School, now over 400 years old, was rebuilt in 1839. (JW)

ABOVE: Elmdon School was in the end cottage (nearest the camera) of this row. Known as Elmdon Terrace, it was close to the Hall. (JW) BELOW: The cottage in School Lane, Solihull, built to house Martha Palmer's School in 1830. (SL)

ABOVE: Hampton Boys' with the master, W.A. Frodin, and his assistant, outside the school in 1912. The building is now used as the Library. (SL) BELOW: Hampton Girls' and Infants School c1906. (SL) OPPOSITE: LEFT: The title page of Richard Jago's poem, *Edge-Hill.* RIGHT: Richard Jago's signature, written in 1744 when he was the curate at Lapworth. BELOW: Lime Tree House, better known as the Manor House, Solihull c1910. Here John Powell is thought to have had his school before moving to The Priory. (SL) CENTRE: An advertisement of 1935.

EDGE-HILL,

OR,

THE RURAL PROSPECT

DELINEATED AND MORALIZED.

A

POEM.

In FOUR BOOKS.

By RICHARD JAGO, A.M.

" Salve, magna parens frugum, Saturnia tellus,
" Magna virum! tibi res antiquæ laudis, et artes
" Ingredior, sanctos ausus recludere fontes."
VIRG.

LONDON,

subscribed our names
R. Jago.

ABOVE: Catherine de Barnes school-cum-church was built by Mr Joseph Gillott of New Berry Hall in 1879. (JW) BELOW: Mill Lane Boys' School was built in 1892, on land given by Mr Gillott, to relieve the overcrowding at Park Road. Three classrooms accommodated 100 boys aged 7 and upwards. From 1893 they were obliged to stay until 11 years and from 1899 until 12 years old. (SL)

ABOVE: In this old drawing of Powell's School the boys play in the garden, one group (left) flying a kite. (WCRO) BELOW: Bentley Heath school-cum-church opened in 1870. The £445 it cost to build was bequeathed by Mr George Homer of Solihull. (SL)

ABOVE: The parish accounts of 1534-5 show the income from a Church
Ale. BELOW: The Forest Hall, Meriden, HQ of the Woodmen of Arden.

The Social Circle Gaily Join'd

For ordinary people in the past there was little time for rest and relaxation, their only work-free days being Sundays and certain festivals. Before the Reformation these were usually holy-days when, after church, the day was given over to revelry and fun: dancing, drinking and games, some of which — football, wrestling, cudgel play — were quite rough.

At Easter and Whitsuntide there was often a Church Ale, a form of fête held in the churchyard, the refreshment strong ale, which encouraged generous giving. The malt was begged by the churchwardens who then brewed vast quantities. Sold to allcomers, the proceeds went to the upkeep of the church. In 1534 an 'Ale' held at Solihull raised 39s 9d, enough to pay the running expenses of St Alphege for an average year.

A special day of celebration was 1 May, mummers with hobby-horses parading the streets, performing short plays, acting out in dumb show Robin Hood and Maid Marion and Lord and Lady of the May. There were also giants, Morris men, games and dancing round the flower-bedecked maypole. At Solihull, where such revels continued into the 19th century, there was Jack-in-the-Green. Made to appear extra tall, Jack wore a costume covered with ivy, holly and evergreens and danced round the streets collecting money. He was accompanied by the chimney sweeps who dressed up in fantastic costumes, one of them wearing a golden crown. This harmless fun was brought to an end, as were the various fairs, by Canon Evans, rector 1872-94, who disapproved of the noise and the spectators it attracted from Birmingham. The maypole was allowed and continued at Solihull until c1910 and in many other local villages until c1940.

At Knowle on the eve and morning of May Day, in the ancient and traditional way, the children picked quantities of wild flowers; these were bound into garlands and decorated the maypole newly set up outside the Greswolde. In the afternoon the children danced, played games, had tea. The revels were not disturbed by traffic until 1919 when they moved elsewhere.

The annual fairs at Balsall, Hampton, Meriden and Solihull, which lasted from three to eight days, coincided with saints' days. Although these were chiefly trading days it was a chance to relax, to meet friends, to eat, drink and exchange news. There were side shows and probably fencing, jumping, skittles, quoits, cock-fighting, bull-baiting and similar 'sports'. Visitors could stay at the local inns which, until the 17th century, rarely had names, the exceptions being the Swanne at Solihull, first mentioned in 1583, and the Cokke and Swann at Knowle mentioned in 1542. There were also numerous alehouses and taverns, for many people brewed ale, the common drink for all ages and classes. The standard and measure of ale sold (like that of bread) was regulated by tasters appointed by each manor court. The brewing of sub-standard ale was a common offence for which five Solihull women were fined in 1514. At the same court, for the same crime 12 other women and a man, described as 'common tipplers' meaning that they sold ale only in a small way, were also fined. At the same time three innkeepers — Henry Warren, Thomas Cordes, both of Solihull, and Ralph Botte of Shirley Street (his inn perhaps being on the site of the Red Lion) — were fined for taking excessive profit.

For the gentry there was ample leisure time, much of which was spent in the saddle, riding, hawking and hunting. The villagers were forbidden such sport or even to keep 'hunting' animals; at Solihull in 1544 it was 'ordered no inhabitant shall keep greyhounds, odorous ferrets or the variety of dogs called Spaniels who does not hold land to the value of 40s', a qualification which cut out all but the better-off. But all men were supposed to know how to shoot, it being 'ordained that every inhabitant shall have bows and arrows ... and is ordered to use them', practising at the butts regularly as part of the obligation to serve in the local militia. As bows fell out of use in favour of guns, archery became a lost art until revived as a sport for gentlemen in the 18th century.

At the Reformation many festivals were dropped from the calendar but on the remaining days there was still much merrymaking. Those who wished for a more Puritan way of life deplored such revelry and in 1603 Church Ales, the frequent cause of drunken brawls, were forbidden. Yet brawls continued, being the most common disturbance, disagreement and arguments often settled with fisticuffs and drawn blood. At Solihull minor cases were heard in the manor court where fines of between 20d and 3s 4d were imposed. When John Ashurst and George Grissold fought in 1631 they were each fined 2s but when Grissold had a second fight, this time with Ralph Randall, he was fined 3s 4d.

More serious cases went to the Quarter Sessions, the people of Balsall, Berkswell and Solihull being the ones who quarrelled most. Balsall, despite its small population, had the worst record, 35 people being fined in the 15 years 1635-50 for offences — stealing, poaching, forcible entry, assault — against 14 of their neighbours. In 1635 Thomas Ryton assaulted John Arche, a weaver; Arche with two friends then attacked Ryton. Clearly of a violent nature, Ryton twice attacked other men. He then moved to Berkswell where he worked as a labourer and also kept an alehouse, being fined in 1641 for having no licence. Having obtained a licence, Ryton reformed and in 1646 was described by the minister and churchwardens as 'of good behaviour and fit to continue with his ale house'.

The Edwards family of Balsall was also hot-tempered. Thomas and Nicholas were blacksmiths and Nicholas also kept 'an ancient inn', perhaps the George-in-the-Tree, described as 'very fit for entertaining of passengers either horsemen or footmen'. His licence, suppressed for a time, was renewed in 1636 after his neighbours agreed 'he hath behaved himself' but in 1641 he was fined for selling less than a quart of best beer for 1d. Later, with his wife Ann, daughter Mary and others, Edwards was involved in separate cases of 'assault and riot' on two women and George Hicken, a tailor.

Generally the 1640s was a violent decade, as soldiers of both sides in the Civil War moved back and forth across the Midlands. There was a constant demand on the villages and towns for money, food, horses, carts and shelter. A rare record has survived revealing how Berkswell suffered. Close to Coventry and Kenilworth, both in Parliamentary hands, the people paid various taxes, loans and subsidies: for horses, soldiers' wages etc. Soldiers and their horses were often 'free-quartered' on the inhabitants, Francis Forrest keeping 23 men and 15 horses on one occasion. The troops requisitioned what they needed and plundered what they wanted.

As people began to travel more, inns grew in importance and more acquired names. Among the named local inns in the 17th century were the Red Lion and the Bell at Meriden (both recorded in the Hearth Tax Return of 1662) and 'the sign of the Cock' at Elmdon kept in 1672 by Francis Hobby. At Solihull James Russhen kept an inn, probably the present George Hotel, the core of which is mediaeval and may have been a hostelry for centuries. A probate inventory taken at Russhen's death in 1667 reveals that some rooms, probably his own quarters, were finely furnished. In the pantry were large quantities of pewter: dishes, flagons, spoons and chamber pots, and in the buttery 12 hogsheads of home-brewed beer, each holding $52\frac{1}{2}$ (imperial) gallons. An upper room called the Bell Chamber may have given the inn its name, the George being known as the Bell in 1693. Russhen lived in Solihull throughout the Civil War and Commonwealth, taking his share of parish duties as Surveyor of the Highways for the Borough. It is possible that he witnessed the arrival of Charles I in Solihull in October 1642, where he was joined by Prince Rupert. The Prince, on his way from Stourbridge with captured mounted guns, had skirmished at Kings Norton with Lord Willoughby and lost 70 men. A few days later the battle of Edgehill took place.

Inns also became increasingly important in village life being convivial meetings places where, as parish government increased, churchwardens, overseers of the poor, constables and highway surveyors could gather to administer affairs. At Knowle in the early 18th century 2s 6d was spent on ale (approximately 60 pints) at most parish meetings, while the overseers, discussing apprenticing in 1706, 'spent at ye Lyon ... setting out Neelers boy 1s 8d'. An unknown crisis in the Neeler family had thrown them on the parish. The Knowle overseers spent £17 (about 25% of the annual poor budget) feeding, clothing and caring for the Neelers and apprenticing Edmund, aged eight, in Birmingham and his sister Alice, aged 11, locally. It took numerous meetings and at least three visits to Birmingham to deal with this one family. Yet food and ale were the only reward given to those who (often unwillingly if chosen by rota) spent their days and free time on unpaid parish business. Perks at a Hampton meeting in 1723 were 'Tobacco and Candles 4s 8d'.

The parish constables, also unpaid, were continually busy: observing strangers, moving on undesirables, and journeying, particularly to Warwick with official lists, monies and to court. It was common practice to lodge suspects held in temporary custody at a local inn at the parish's expense. George Stitch *alias* Ashton was held at the George, Solihull in June 1758 on his way to Warwick Gaol, three guards sitting with him all night. Joined by two other men, they ate 11 meals at 4d each and drank 7s worth of ale (again about 60 pints) before taking Stitch to prison; horse hire, turnpikes and more ale brought the total cost to 21s.

The establishment of bowling-greens at inns from the late 17th century onwards added an extra attraction. Probably the oldest known locally is that at the George, Solihull, reputedly made in 1693 when Dog Lane Croft was added to the property. Although a popular and ancient game, bowls was forbidden for many centuries as it interfered with archery practice. Private greens were permitted by licence in the 16th century but it was not until after 1688 that playing bowls was generally allowed at inns. In time greens were established at the Swan, the Red Lion, the Greswolde at Knowle, the Forest at Dorridge, the George-in-the-Tree at Balsall Common, the Saracen's Head at Shirley, the Bradford Arms at Castle Bromwich; the game enjoying great popularity in the 19th century when competitions and leagues were instituted. At Solihull a slightly different game is played to other clubs; any bowls overrunning the jack by six feet are discounted, special sticks being kept to measure the distance.

In 1790 William Jones, the assistant bowling-green keeper at Solihull, died of pneumonia. He requested that, after his funeral, his bearers should play a game of bowls. At the time gentlemen and clergy from a wide area met together convivially and played bowls at the George, among them the rector, Rev Charles Curtis, who was also rector of St Martin's, Birmingham (1781-1829). A fine example of a rich sporting parson and a strong Tory, he had a nationally reported dispute with the passionate Whig clergyman, Dr Samuel Parr of Hatton. They met at Solihull bowling-green in September 1791 and comments concerning Dr Joseph Priestley, whose house and fine library had recently been destroyed in the Birmingham riots, brought the ill-feeling to a head.

Curtis was also an early member of the Woodmen of Arden, an archery club founded by a group of local gentlemen, including the Earl of Aylesford, Mr York of Kingshurst, Henry Greswold Lewis of Malvern Hall and William Bree, vicar of Bickenhill at the Bulls Head, Meriden (later Darlaston Hall) in November 1785. Members met to shoot every Monday and Friday from Easter to October and dined regularly during the winter. The subscription was one guinea and the uniform of green coat, white waistcoat and breeches, with the Arden button, was to be worn all at meetings. Initially shooting took place at the Bulls Head or on Meriden Heath, but an archery ground was soon acquired where butts and the Forest Hall, designed by the architect Bonomi, were established by 1788. Situated in Meriden Road the Hall, now greatly extended, is still the Society's headquarters, where shooting still takes place. There are no lady members, but since 1829 female visitors have had their targets (at 60 yards) and compete for a variety of awards. During its first century 473 clergymen and gentlemen joined the Woodmen and the families of many of them still continue their association. The number of members is restricted to 80; the Warden has always been the Earl of Aylesford.

Charles Curtis resigned from the Woodmen in 1788, for his great passion was riding to hounds. When he came to Solihull in 1789 there was no organized local hunt, but many country gentlemen had a few hounds and with neighbours hunted the fox and hare in the local countryside, where there was still much woodland as well as considerable unenclosed common land. The Meriden area was hunted from 1778 by Mr John Corbet, his foxhound Trojan being famous in the annals of hunting. In 1791, with Corbet as Master, the Warwickshire Hunt came into being, Curtis being an enthusiastic supporter. The whole county was hunted, the kennels being at Meriden and at Stratford. The meets were early in the morning, the fox traced by his 'drag', the route he had taken on his return from his previous night's foraging. A hunt club was established at the White Lion, Stratford, where merry post-hunting evenings were spent and quantities of port consumed; an evening uniform of scarlet coat with gilt buttons and a black velvet collar was worn.

In 1811 the new master of the Warwickshire, Lord Middleton, closed the Meriden Kennels and hunting in this area — 'the finest woodland in the world' — ceased. It may have been from that time that Curtis employed his own huntsman, Joe Pitchford, and kept a pack of harriers in kennels in Drury Lane, chasing chiefly the hare, but occasionally the fox. Curtis is reputed to have had a fox served as a supper dish at the Rectory. He is said to have told Pitchford 'If you catch him, I'll eat him.' The fox was caught, taken home and if not eaten, 'toasted' at table. A man of similar tastes was John Burman, a contemporary who lived at Light Hall, Shirley. His hounds were kept in Dog Kennel Lane, from which it takes its name.

In 1832 Mr Robert Vyner established a pack of hounds and hunted in north Warwickshire; the following season he hunted the Solihull coverts with 30 couples of hounds then moved to Leamington. Later both the Atherstone and Warwickshire Hunts were in the district, Mr Wilson of Knowle Hall being the Master for two seasons. He also had his own drag hounds. Wilson's passion for hunting caused him to spend two fortunes and die penniless; he pulled down most of Knowle Hall as too expensive to repair. In 1853 a permanent Hunt, the North Warwickshire, was finally established, many local gentlemen — Mr Muntz of Umberslade, Rev Mynors of St Patricks, Salter Street, the Burman family, Mr Robinson of Hockley Heath, Mr Walker of Packwood, the Lant family of Nailcote Hall, Mr Boultbee of Springfield Hall — being enthusiasts. The hounds were more important than the horses, Richard Lant paying £950 for 50 couple when he became Master in 1868. After the First War army horses were sold off locally and this made it possible for more farmers and ordinary countrymen to follow the hounds. Meets were held throughout the area but particularly in Berkswell at the Hall (where the stirrup cup was served by the butler and footman), and in the village, at Westwood Heath, at Solihull in the Square and at the station, at Shirley, Knowle, Packwood, Umberslade and at Tanworth which was particularly good hunting country. The increase in heavy traffic and the growth of motorways made hunting increasingly difficult and in 1985 the North Warwickshire was disbanded.

In 1798 Parson Curtis and other men of Solihull, Knowle and Elmdon, anxious about the war with France, proposed forming a Troop of Horse. It was to supplement the militia, the official Home Guard, to which each parish was obliged to send men at its own expense, Solihull's quota being seven. Commanded by 'Captain' Harding and 'Lieutenant' Chattock, both solicitors, the 38 named privates — Curtis, innkeepers, tradesmen and farmers — each agreed to provide their own horse, arms and uniform of leather breeches, blue frock, red cape and waistcoat, round hat with feather and yellow buttons marked S.K. & E.A. In August 1803, as invasion threatened, the Solihull Volunteers were mustered under Harding and Chattock. By December 132 men from

Solihull, Knowle, Hampton and Barston had enrolled, although the corps was not quite as originally envisaged and Curtis was not a member. They served regularly until 1805 when the crisis was over.

Bowls, archery and hunting were not for everyone but horse racing crossed social boundaries. About 1830 annual races were begun in Solihull, the course, 35½ acres in extent, being in the Warwick/Ashleigh Road area. Owned by Lt Thomas Chattock, now a large landowner, the land was let to Hugh Taylor, landlord of the George and Joseph Findon. Initially well attended, the Flat Races consisted of three events each with an average field of six runners, but after 1840 the course is not mentioned. Another course is shown on a map of 1886; called Packington Race Course it was on Meriden Heath. It soon ceased and by 1895 had become a golf course. Much more successful was Shirley Race Course, now Shirley Golf Club, probably started in the mid-19th century on land owned by the Horton family of Elliott's Hall. They were keen on racing and had a viewing stand built onto the house. Racing, which included some steeplechasing, continued at Shirley until 1953 (with a break 1939-45) and at least two stands were erected for spectators. The course was popular, the Master at Shirley School recording in the school Log Book of 1907 that 'many children are absent as their parents are afraid to let them be on the road on Shirley Race Day on account of the traffic.'

In the early 19th century Shirley was known as a place of ill-repute chiefly because of the sporting activities at the Plume of Feathers inn. Here a rough element, mostly from Birmingham, congregated to enjoy prize fighting, bull-baiting (abolished 1835), and cock-fighting (abolished 1839) which continued for a time illegally. The chapel-of-ease opened in 1831 opposite the Plume was no deterrent to the sporting fraternity, who continued to gather there, the Constable and Chapel-warden attempting to catch a party of men watching an illegal dog-fight at the inn in 1842.

For those who enjoyed quieter pursuits cricket was gaining popularity with local gentlemen, who met occasionally to play. In July 1838 Archer Clive rode over to Meriden to play for three hours before lunch. By the 1850s Solihull Cricket Club had been formed and was highly successful. Its members, all gentlemen, came from a wide area and included the Alstons from Elmdon Hall, John Lant from Berkswell and Lord Guernsey, who sported a pork-pie cap of gipsy colours above his whites. There was also a club called 'The Knickerbockers', named from their white flannel nether garments, which they wore with red stockings.

About 1870 village club cricket became a Saturday afternoon diversion, men of all social classes enjoying the game together. Among the earliest to be founded locally were Hampton in 1871, Shirley in 1873 (the subscription being 5s per annum), Olton in 1888 and Berkswell in 1896. Knowle had two clubs — Knowle Village, which played in Hampton Lane, and Knowle and Dorridge, which still plays at its pleasant ground in Station Road. Solihull played Knowle at home on 16 July 1881, each side making 43. Later in the season, which continued to the end of September, Solihull played Dorridge, and Knowle and District. Olton and Berkswell both had members who played for England: William Quaife, who lived in Kineton Green Road, from 1910-51, and Bob Wyatt, who cut his cricket teeth on bumpy local pitches while living at Carol Green. Will Quaife ran a cricket school and had a bat-making business at Olton, the latter in partnership with Dick Lilley, another England player.

At Berkswell there were also lady cricketers: Maud and Lilian Watson, the daughters of the rector. The Watsons were keen tennis players as well, practising regularly on their own courts at the Rectory. In 1884 they met each other at Wimbledon where Maud, the younger, became the first Ladies' Champion. At the time many houses had courts, and tennis parties were a regular facet of middle-class social life. The oldest club in the district is the Solihull Lawn Tennis Club, founded in 1873, which for many years was in Homer Road. As tennis increased in popularity more clubs were started; by 1906 tennis and croquet lawns were established at the George-in-the-Tree, Balsall Common, and in time, in many public parks.

Energetic relaxation was very much the vogue in the late 19th century; cricket, tennis, football, golf and 'cycling all gained devotees. The first Warwickshire golf club opened in 1886 just when the modern safety bicycle was being developed. A number of local golf clubs were founded in the 1890s, The Arden being the first in Greater Solihull. Its nine-hole course was laid out in 1891 on fields at the corner of Streetsbrook and Sharmans Cross Roads. The following year Robin Hood, another nine-hole course, was founded between Lakey Lane and Stratford Road; it had a ladies' club attached, an advanced idea. In 1893 J.P. Heaton, who had been a member of Robin Hood, started a new club at Olton, on land beside Dovehouse Lane. The course, extended to 18 holes in 1895, was considered difficult as a stream runs through it. A farmhouse on the property, Olton House, was used as a clubhouse. It was pleasant and comfortable and the ladies' section was able to have its own quarters. Later, when the surrounding land started to be developed, a new clubhouse was built in Heaton Road. The North Warwickshire Club, on the well-drained soil of Meriden Heath, began in 1895 as a nine-hole course and gained the reputation of being playable even in the wettest weather. The following year another nine-hole course was laid out at Castle Bromwich. In 1910 the last of the early local clubs, Copt Heath, was founded on land surrounding Longdon Hall, once part of the estate of Lady Byron. A fine new clubhouse with excellent facilities was opened in the 1970s. In the 1930s a short-lived club opened at Chadwick Manor, and Shirley opened in the 1950s.

While the middle-classes were joining golf clubs, all classes were taking to the open road as 'cycling became a craze. A 'bike' made it possible for people from the towns to enjoy exercise, fresh air and discover the countryside. In particular it enabled women to get about alone, a freedom they had never previously enjoyed. Clubs were formed — there was an early one in Solihull — members travelling quite long distances. People from Birmingham were particularly drawn to Shirley but the whole area attracted 'cycling visitors. Publicans and country cottagers quickly realised the potential and many started providing light refreshments, 'Teas' being painted in large letters on roofs and sign boards. Inns, their premises under-used since the advent of the railway, made 'cyclists welcome for meals and overnight stops.

After the First War the National Memorial to 'cyclists killed in action was erected on the green at Meriden. It was unveiled in 1921 by Lord Birkenhead, with thousands of 'cyclists present. Each year in May a service of remembrance is held at Meriden, people travelling from all over England.

Until 1939 the small airfield at Castle Bromwich was the only one in Greater Solihull. The first 'plane landed there in 1909 and subsequently many air race flyers put down there. It continued in use until 1958. Early flyers put down almost anywhere and Edwin Prosser of Moseley regularly flew from fields behind the Saracen's Head at Shirley until Dr Coole Kneale, who lived close by, objected. Later in 1933, Alan Cobham and his flying circus organized short cheap flights for the public from an 'airfield' in Longmore Road, Shirley.

During the 1920s a completely new entertainment entered people's lives — the cinema. Picture houses opened in many towns and villages, although not all of them were able to keep going through the 'thirties. Ye Arden Cinema, Solihull opened in 1926, the manageress wearing evening dress to receive her patrons; the seats upstairs were 1s 6d and downstairs 9d and 6d. Known for many years as Solihull Cinema, it has closed recently, to the regret of many. Other early cinemas were the Palace Picture House, Balsall, opened in 1925 and later known as The Cameo, and the Picture Playhouse, Knowle. Olton Cinema opened in 1934 and the Odeon, Shirley in 1936.

ABOVE: The Red Lion, Shirley, its name board on the roof, in the 1920s. Partially rebuilt in 1937, it was demolished in 1967 and a new Red Lion was erected further back from the road. (SL) BELOW: The Cock, Coventry Road, Elmdon, a 17th century building demolished for road widening. (SL)

ABOVE: The Red Lion and White Swan Inns, Knowle c1890, the latter taken down c1939 and its timbers stored in a field. (JW) BELOW: The roof and bowling green at the George, Solihull, from the church tower in the 1930s. The houses in George Road are being built and beyond are fields and trees. (SL)

ABOVE: Knowle Hall in 1829 before Mr W.H.B.J. Wilson pulled much of it down. BELOW: Berkswell Hall, rebuilt in 1812 by John Eardley Eardley Wilmot. Later extended, by 1887 the house had 19 principal bedrooms with 11 for the servants. (SL)

The Solihull Volunteers,

AGREED UPON

At a General Meeting held the 5th of October, 1803.

I. THE Commanding Officer shall appoint the Time and Place of every General Meeting for Exercise.

II. Officers, having Charge of any Division or Number, shall appoint (subject to the Control of the Commanding Officer) the Hours and Place of Drill.

III. Every Member of this Corps shall attend punctually at the Time and Place appointed for Exercise or Drill: and at every General Meeting, and at such other Times as the Commanding Officer shall direct, shall appear in his Uniform, and with his Person, Dress, Arms, and Accoutrements, clean and in good Order.

IV. The Roll shall, by the Direction of the senior Officer in Rank present, be called over Five Minutes after the Time appointed for Meeting; and every Member not then present (and having no sufficient Excuse to be allowed by the Commanding Officer) shall forfeit, if the Commanding Officer, *Five Shillings;* if any other Commissioned Officer, *Two Shillings and Sixpence;* if a Sergeant, *Sixpence;* if a private Member, *Threepence;* and every Member (not having a sufficient Excuse to be allowed as before) who shall not appear in his Place, within a Quarter of an Hour, from the Time of Meeting, shall pay Double the above Penalties.

V. Every Member who shall not attend with his Person, Clothes, Arms, and Accoutrements, clean and in good Order, to the Satisfaction of the Commanding Officer present, shall not be suffered to join the Ranks, and shall pay the same Fine as in Case of Absence.

VI. In all Cases of Absence; a second, and each succeeding Offence, till the Member shall have attended in his Place, shall be punished by a double Fine.

VII. On the Certificate of the Commanding Officer that any Member is sufficiently qualified, such Member shall not be required to attend future Drills.

VIII. The Commanding Officer may grant Leave of Absence for sufficient Reason, to be judged of by him.

IX. Every Member who shall not, during the Time of Exercise and whilst on Duty, be silent, attentive, orderly, and obedient to the Commands of his Officers; shall, for each Offence, pay a Fine of *One Shilling.* All Offences against this Article to be determined by the Commanding Officer present.

X. Every Member who shall, whilst on Duty, be guilty of any Misbehaviour not expressly provided against by the preceding Articles, shall pay a Fine not exceeding *Two Shillings and Sixpence,* nor lefs than *One Shilling,* according to the Nature of the Offence; to be determined by the Officer commanding at the Time when the Offence shall be committed.

XI. Every Member who shall wear his Uniform, except on Duty or with the Permission of his Captain, shall pay a Fine of *Two Shillings and Sixpence;* except those providing their own Uniform.

XII. The Captain of the Company may, for any Cause which shall appear to him sufficient, discharge any Member of the Corps.

XIII. No Member shall leave the Corps, or cease to be a Member thereof, unless discharged in Manner directed by the preceding Article, upon Pain of forfeiting as follows, *viz.* if a Commissioned Officer, *Twenty Pounds,* and if any other Member *Ten Pounds.*

The regulations of the Solihull Volunteers, formed during the Napoleonic War. (SL)

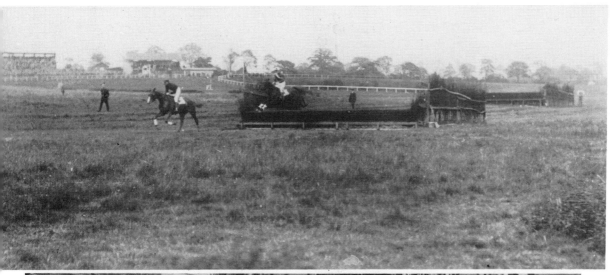

ABOVE: Shirley Race Course in the 1920s (ROS) BELOW: The Plume of Feathers, Shirley c1910, when it had lost its bad reputation. The lady 'cyclist is thought to be Mabel Wilson, the landlord's daughter. (JM)

ABOVE: The Castle Inn, Castle Bromwich, which village people frequented, since they were not welcome at the coaching inns. It is now a shop — Castle Stores. (SL) BELOW: The Ring O' Bells, Hampton, kept in 1902 by James Tall, previously butler at the Hall. The name is now associated with the adjacent garage. (SL)

LEFT: The Cyclists' Memorial, Meriden. (JW) RIGHT: The Cross and Well House, Berkswell, takes its name from its proximity to both. For centuries it was the rectory where Maud and Lilian Watson lived. (SL) BELOW: Many young people joined the Scouts and Guides. A parade of both march past Suffield's hardware shop, Stratford Road in the 1930s. (ROS)

ABOVE: Solihull Football Club, founded in 1891, had three most successful seasons 1912-14. The players above, front row: Johnson, Berry, Tarplee, Watts, Thompson; middle row: Hutchinson, Hatwood, Shepherd, Bragg, Coton, Reynolds. (SL) BELOW: While the men enjoyed football, their mothers and wives joined church Women's Meetings: Rev C.O.R. Wormald with Mrs Hamilton Smith (seated second from right) and her group outside Catherine de Barnes school. (SL)

ABOVE: The Picture Playhouse, Station Road, Knowle 1928, from 1931-54
it was known as the Rex Cinema. In May 1955 it became Johnson's Garage.
(AC) BELOW: Olton Cinema, Warwick Road, designed by H.G. Bradley
& Clarke, was demolished in the 1970s and replaced by offices. (JW)

ABOVE: New Berry Hall, Solihull, built by Joseph Gillott junior c1870. Empty since 1957, the house is now a ruin, the fine gardens neglected. (DG) BELOW: Chadwick Manor, built in 1875 of brick in Jacobean style, for many years was a hotel; it is now divided into flats. (JM)

Peopled Streets and Active Industry

Throughout the 19th century the villages of Greater Solihull, like much of Solihull itself, remained wholly rural, although they too attracted a number of successful businessmen and their families, escaping the smoke of Birmingham. By 1870 several villages had a station but, in a pre-'cycle and -car era, commuting was only for those able to walk or be taken to the station. Wealthy men such as Joseph Feeney (owner of the *Birmingham Post and Mail*), Joseph Gillott (pen-nib maker), and a member of the Pears family (soap manufacturers) bought farms later known respectively as The Moat, Berkswell; New Berry Hall and Chadwick Manor. They remodelled the houses or built anew, grandly with turrets, landscaping the grounds. They were accepted into society, often becoming local benefactors.

Much depended on the existing landowners, several of whom had extensive estates: Lord Aylesford owned much of Bickenhill and Meriden, the Earl of Bradford Castle Bromwich, the Alston family Elmdon, the Wykeham-Martin family Packwood, and considerable acreages were held by other large landowners at Temple Balsall, Berkswell, Tanworth, Marston Green, Solihull, and Hampton, where Sir Frederick Peel was very much the squire. He inherited the manor from his father, Sir Robert, a former Prime Minister. Later he engaged architect Eden Nesfield to restore the Church, build new village houses and Hampton Manor (now a home for the mentally handicapped), the workmen being billeted on his tenants. Peel demanded deference, curtsies and raised caps and permitted no-one to walk before him, yet he could be generous, lending his grounds for school treats and similar events.

Generally land for building appears only to have been available in small quantities except at Dorridge and Olton, both places owing their development to the railway. By 1877 Dorridge had grown large enough to need its own church, St Phillip's being built in Manor Road. Originally able to seat 120, it was extended in 1894. At Olton the sale of William William's estate led to the development of St Bernard's and Kineton Green Roads. Sold as building plots, only houses costing £500 plus, then a considerable sum, could be erected. By 1880 Olton was a fashionable residential area peopled by middle-class families: doctors, architects, manufacturers of articles such as guns, jewellery, silver, pens, and their many servants. When Olton was made a parish in 1881, the newly opened church at once proved too small and was extended in 1895. As the population grew, schools were started — a church school in 1885 and a number of private ones. There was considerable social life and several clubs — tennis, cricket, golf, fishing, shooting, sailing — were formed. Later in the century small groups of modest villas were built in the Richmond Road/Castle Lane area, the occupants often working as gardeners and coachmen at the bigger houses.

At the 1869 sale Bernard Ullathorne, the first Catholic Bishop of Birmingham, bought Folly Hall (now St Bernard's Grange) and 42 acres of land. On this he built St Bernard's Seminary for the training of priests. It closed in 1889 and was sold to the Franciscans for a Friary. Services for lay Catholics were held, but not until 1929 was a parishioners' church built.

A Congregational church was opened in Kineton Green Road in 1901. The initial design, which proved too expensive, was by W.H. Bidlake, an Arts and Crafts architect. Art Nouveau was popular in Olton and a number of the houses contain work in this style, in particular stained glass. Many artists were attracted to Olton and it was in Kineton Green Road that Edith Holden lived and wrote her now famous diaries.

Agriculture and its related trades continued to be the major occupation in Greater Solihull; several water-mills still operated, although by 1890 most windmills had ceased to sail, a few converting to steam power. Of the long-established trades, tanning, weaving, and wick-yarn making had gone but there were numerous brickworks and Robinsons, the rake makers, continued to employ 40-50 men in their timber-yard at Hockley Heath. At Meriden Francis Skidmore made high quality metalwork in gold, silver, brass and iron, many churches, the Albert Memorial, and St Pancras Station being enriched by his work. The newest industry, however, was the manufacture of aluminium at Crown Works, Solihull Lodge by James Fern Webster, a pioneer in gas engineering, and a steel and bronze manufacturer. In 1871 he discovered how to produce aluminium in tons rather than ounces, and at a price that made it a commercial proposition. Webster, a secretive man, carried out his experiments at his Edgbaston home and was granted over 200 patents. He sold his Birmingham steel-making works and patent for £96,000, moved to Shirley, and in 1877 built Crown Works; the process was patented in 1881. A syndicate, the Aluminium Company Ltd, was formed in 1887 and Webster was paid £240,000 for his patent; the business later moved to Oldbury. Webster died in 1904, aged 83.

The railway and, as the century turned, the bicycle brought more townspeople into the countryside, but on the whole the houses that were built from 1900 to 1914 were for those employing at least one servant. Packwood, Balsall Common, Hampton had a sprinkling as did Shirley, where the small community, feeling rather isolated, joined together in 1903 to erect an Institute where they could meet and enjoy dances, concerts and plays. Shirley Station opened in 1908 and the first new road — Burman — was cut in 1911.

During the First War some of the larger houses were used as military hospitals including Springfield House, Knowle; The Hermitage, Solihull; The Rectory, Berkswell; and The Institute, Hampton while officers from the Dominions, on leave or injured, were welcome to stay at The Moat, Berkswell. Many middle-class daughters who had never previously worked became drivers or nurses. Other women made shells or worked on the land, replacing the men who went to war. Before they left for France a visit was often made to a photographer, particularly to Edward Hobbins of Solihull, who captured on glass plates wives and children and many khaki-clad men. Occasionally, Zeppelins flew over, bombs being dropped behind the Red Lion Inn, Shirley, at Box Trees and at Packwood Haugh, then a school, where the windows were broken.

After the war, piecemeal building continued in Solihull and in small amounts in the villages but still chiefly for the better-off, although in a few places smaller houses were erected by the RDC: in Kixley Lane and Hampton Lane, Knowle and Oak Lane, Barston. Despite the break-up of the Elmdon, Digby and other large estates it was not until the mid-1930s that any major change in population took place and then only in the villages within Solihull Urban District.

As war clouds loomed once again, contingency plans were made and in 1939 put into action: Castle Bromwich airfield (now Castle Vale housing estate) was used for training pilots on Spitfires. These were made at a nearby factory (later Fisher and Ludlow); 1,298 'planes were produced in one 18-month period. At Elmdon Airport, opened for civil flying in July 1939, men were trained to fly Lancaster and Stirling bombers. Built at Longbridge, then assembled at a shadow factory at Marston Green (later Metro-Cammell), they were towed to the adjacent airfield. In 1941 two further airfields were opened: one at Hockley Heath, also for training, necessitated the demolition of Box Trees Cottage Farm; the other at Balsall Common was constructed as a fighter station and known as RAF Honiley. Throughout the area there were barrage balloons, observation posts, searchlight batteries, including one in Ravenshaw Lane, and anti-aircraft batteries, one in Berkswell Park. At Balsall Common there was a decoy to attract bombers away from the towns.

Those who were not 'called up' were directed into factories, including some women. At Lode Lane women worked 52 hours per week; the pay for dirty work inspecting engine components for bombers was 1s 2d per hour. After work, the Home Guard, ARP, AFS, Red Cross, firewatching and growing food on every bit of land sent people to bed exhausted and hoping there would not be an air raid. There was some bombing in the area, the worst in Solihull, where 26 people were killed and many seriously injured; two buildings in High Street and a number of houses in Alston Road were destroyed. Birmingham and Coventry suffered frequent attacks yet Greater Solihull was chosen as a haven for London evacuees. In November 1940, when Coventry was repeatedly bombed, the area was awash with people. They slept in schools and village halls and even in cars in the lanes to escape the bombs, the residents of Berkswell and Balsall Common having already taken in as many as they could.

There was no hospital at Solihull despite great efforts to start one and minor operations were usually carried out at home or in a nursing home. In 1939 the infirmary wards at the Workhouse — primitive, dirty, poorly heated, badly equipped — were designated an Emergency Hospital. The local doctors appointed to man it — Donovan, Page, Sankey, surgeon Paul Quinet, anaesthetist Doris Quinet — fitted it out with their own equipment, Dr Quinet lending his X-ray machine and operating table. Later Tudor Grange and Totehill, both in Blossomfield Road, were used as Auxiliary Hospitals for wounded soldiers.

Despite the blackout and the shortages all was not gloom. Cinemas and pubs provided welcome relaxation and there were numerous dances, especially where service personnel were stationed. In 1942 Solihull adopted a destroyer, HMS *Vivacious*, sending comforts to its crew. Two years later 100 officers and men spent a weekend in the town enjoying a party, dance, football match and parade.

In the post-war period, homes and a return to peace-time work were the main preoccupations. During the 1950s and '60s some new houses were built in all the villages and a little small industry was permitted: light engineering at Eastcote and the Coventry side of Berkswell, while at Hockley Heath, Nock Bros, builders, employed 30-40 men, but many people still worked in agriculture.

At Solihull, as the fields separating the town from Sheldon, Elmdon, Shirley and Olton disappeared under houses, the bulk of the new residents worked in Birmingham. The majority travelled by 'bus or train, for not every family had a car and only the better-off had two. As the housing estates went up, junior schools followed and educational opportunities, generally, were greatly improved through new secondary and grammar schools; a campus of five grammar schools and a technical college were built off Blossomfield Road. A wide range of adult evening classes was avilable, and other recreational facilities increased, as swimming, squash and athletics gained in popularity. Several communal groups were also formed as the newcomers, often far away from family and friends, attempted to form fresh bonds.

The war-time Emergency Hospital in the Workhouse became, post-war, Solihull Hospital. In succeeding years many improvements were made but conditions were always difficult and the medical staff looked for a large new hospital to serve the growing population. In the 1950s the hospital's small maternity unit was divided between Brook House and Netherwood, adapted houses in Lode Lane. Applicants were interviewed by the Matron for beds were limited, each new mother staying two weeks. The Netherwood mothers were moved after a day or two to the old isolation hospital at Catherine de Barnes. Built in 1907 by Solihull and Meriden Councils jointly, for patients with notifiable diseases, it was difficult to reach for husbands without a car. When, many years later, a large new wing was added to Solihull Hospital, it housed the long-suffering maternity unit.

In Birmingham the slum clearance and house building programmes, started before the war, resumed as soon as conditions allowed, but by 1963 land shortage was a problem. The city therefore acquired 1,540 acres at Chelmsley Wood, Kingshurst, Marston Green and Castle Bromwich from Warwickshire County Council, on which to build some 1,600 homes with the necessary shops, schools, services, etc. Work started in 1966, when the beautiful and ancient Chelmsley Wood, after which the development was named, was felled. Other names of locally historic interest were used, particularly for the schools; one was named after Simon Digby, whose legacy had helped children to learn 250 years previously. The Queen visited Chelmsley in April 1971 to officially open the shopping centre, a complex of shops, offices, flats, car parks and pubs.

At Kingshurst haphazard private building had started in the 1950s on land near Kingshurst Hall. Plans to turn the Queen Anne house into a community centre fell through for lack of funds and it was demolished in 1962. Until the building of the Chelmsley estates, Kingshurst residents felt isolated and there were complaints about the poor facilities and 'bus services. In 1974 both areas passed to Solihull, when the Metropolitan Borough was formed.

At Elmdon the airport had returned to civil use in 1949 and scheduled services resumed. From 1955 tourist flights increased and subsequently the runway was extended, Coventry Road was widened and some buildings were demolished. In the early 1950s Elmdon Hall, empty for many years, was thought superfluous and pulled down. The park (now public), church and a few old houses remain but little else, the grounds of the Range Rover factory, new roads and houses covering the fields. Recently the airport has been extended into Bickenhill and changed its name to Birmingham International Airport to reflect its increasingly intercontinental role.

Bickenhill too has almost lost its identity, although the village, happily by-passed, remains secluded and unspoilt. Close by is the M42 which joins the M6 near Coleshill, and the much widened and greatly improved old turnpike roads to Coventry, Chester, Kenilworth and Lichfield. In 1970, because of its proximity to the airport and motorway network, Bickenhill was chosen as the site of the NEC, opened by the Queen in 1976. The railway line to Euston, electrified during the 1960s, skirted the site, therefore a new station, Birmingham International, was built to serve the Exhibition Centre. The NEC, a complex including nine halls, hotels, shops and banks, is joined to the station, which is linked to the airport by Maglev, a rapid transport system.

In the 1970s a combination of circumstances — the forming of Solihull Metropolitan Borough, the NEC, the proximity of the motorway network and air and rail transport, plus the demise of part of Birmingham's industry — changed Solihull. More jobs became available within the Borough as offices were built, and clean industry was attracted to the old trading estates and new business parks. This has led to increased house building in Solihull and, together with an increasing wish to live in the country, has had a knock-on effect in the villages. Knowle, Dorridge and Balsall Common have grown enormously, new villages have been created at Cheswick Green and Shelly and, where minimum new building has been allowed, every suitable barn and dilapidated cottage has been converted and restored.

Hampton Manor House, built c1870, described by Pevsner as 'dull, though dignified'.

ABOVE: A home for 'idiot' children, founded in 1866 by two doctors at Dorridge Grove, had grown by 1902 into the Asylum, purpose-built on a new site. By 1948, when the name was changed to Middlefield, there were 270 inmates. (SL) BELOW: One of several attractive houses at Marston Green, now Chelmsley Hospital. They were built c1880 by Birmingham as Marston Green Cottage Homes for orphan and poor children. (JW)

TO LET,

SOLIHULL LODGE, situated on the Highway leading from Solihull to King's Norton, in the County of Warwick ONE SEMI-DETACHED RESIDENCE, recently erected (in the Gothic style), regardless of expense, and suited to the requirements of large families. Pleasantly situated in a proverbially healthy district, five miles from Birmingham, $2\frac{1}{2}$ miles from the Moseley and King's Heath Stations on the Midland Railway, three miles from the Solihull Station on the Great Western Railway, and within a few minutes' walk from Yardley Wood Church.

The house contains a spacious Entrance Hall, Dining Room, 18 feet 6 inches by 15 feet; Drawing Room, 18 feet by 15 feet, with bay window; Breakfast Room, 12 feet by 15 feet; China and Cook's Pantries; Kitchens and Cellars. On the first floor—five Chambers, Dressing Room, Store Closet, W.C., and Laundry; second floor—four Bed Rooms and Store Closet. The Out-buildings comprise Stabling for two horses; Carriage House, with loft over, &c. The residence stands a pleasant distance from the road, with tastefully laid-out Grounds, having excellent Kitchen Gardens, containing choice Fruit Trees, and Pleasure Grounds at the rear, with three acres of Pasture Land if required.

GRIMLEY AND SONS,

Temple Street,

BIRMINGHAM.

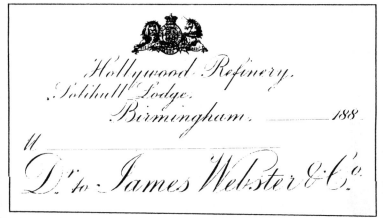

PATENT METAL PAINT AND COLOUR WORKS,
42 & 43, OOZELLS STREET,
Birmingham, 18

M

Bought of JAMES WEBSTER & CO.,

SOLE PATENTEES & MANUFACTURERS OF THE PATENT METAL PAINT.

THIS PAINT IS A POSITIVE PROTECTOR TO IRON, AND IS APPLICABLE TO ALL KINDS OF MATERIALS, AND MAY BE HAD IN VARIOUS COLOURS.

PRIZE

HAVRE.

		T.	C.	Q.	lb.	Price.	£	s.	d.

Hollywood Refinery,
Solihull Lodge,
Birmingham, 188

M

Dr to James Webster & Co.

Two bill heads of James Fern Webster's businesses, and an advertisement letting a house at Solihull Lodge. He probably lived in the adjoining house.
(RS)

108

ABOVE: Priory Mill and pool, Solihull Lodge c1913, for a time, late last century, was a needle mill. (JM) BELOW: The Congregational Church, Olton, now the United Reformed Church. (SL)

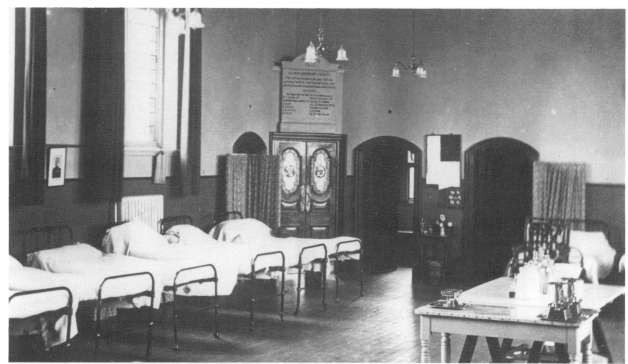

OPPOSITE ABOVE: Hampton-in-Arden Institute in use as a hospital in the First World War. (SL) LEFT: Doris Hamilton Smith worked as a nurse at The Hermitage in the First World War. (SL) RIGHT: A Solihull mother and her children photographed by Edward Hobbins, perhaps for father to take to war. (DG) ABOVE: The Webb family of Deebanks Yard, Warwick Road, Solihull, also photographed by Hobbins. Soldier Jack Webb was in The Royal Warwickshire's City Battalion. (DG) BELOW: Council houses at Oak Lane, Barston, built between the wars. (JW)

ABOVE: Mr Harry Wood shoes a horse at the smithy which stood on the corner of Longmore and Stratford Roads. Work ceased in the late 1930s; the shop and adjacent cottage were demolished in 1956. (AW) BELOW: Members of the crew of HMS *Vivacious* enjoy a party in the British Restaurant, Mill Lane, Solihull in March 1944. The ship, a 'V/W' Class destroyer, was built at Yarrow in 1917 and sold in 1947. (SL)

ABOVE: Post-war houses in the Marsh Lane estate, Hampton. (SL) BELOW:
The buildings at the back of Solihull Hospital, once part of the Workhouse,
before modernisation, c1950/60s. (SL)

ABOVE: Birmingham International Station. (JW) RIGHT: Redwood House, a block of flats at Kingshurst. (JW) BELOW: Maglev: using frictionless magnetic suspension, the car travels along an elevated track from the station to the airport, 600 metres, in 90 seconds. (In 1983, it won the prestigious Viva Award of the City of London's Guild of Carmen of which the publisher is a Past Master.) (JW)

Not to Trust to Transient Dreams

Since work on this book began Solihull town has changed considerably. A new road has appeared, a five storey hotel plus several large office blocks have sprung up and major changes are due in the centre. Shirley too has altered and in places is hardly recognisable. The Stratford Road (now dubbed the Golden Mile) has been widened and has sprouted roundabouts, restaurants, supermarkets, a large multi-screen cinema and Monkspath Business Park.

The Draft Development Plan for the Borough to the year 2001, published in January 1990, shows that new houses are planned at Meriden, Balsall Common, Hampton, Knowle, Dorridge (already started), Hockley Heath, Catherine de Barnes, Dickens Heath and Solihull. In some of these places small business sites are also zoned, the largest being beside the M42 on land anciently farmed by the Sidenhales. New by-passes are outlined for Hockley Heath, Knowle and Balsall Common, while at Berkswell the prospect of the coal-mine still threatens. The area to the north of the Coventry Road is almost wholly given over to the airport, NEC and business parks with some new housing to supplement the existing stock.

Many residents are deeply disturbed by the amount of building which has already taken place and fear the loss of further open spaces and the erosion of the Green Belt. Business and finance are sometimes thought to receive more attention and consideration than the inhabitants of the Borough. Yet the Local Authority is not altogether a free agent, for the requirements of the Secretary of State and the West Midlands generally have to be met. Circumstances, not choice, have placed Solihull at the hub of the motorway system, and the business world, not unnaturally, wishes to utilize this advantage. Some co-operation is necessary for the Borough to survive but business parks with adjoining pleasure parks, landscaped river banks and golf courses are not the same as natural countryside.

And it should not go unnoticed that Birmingham International Airport, Birmingham International Station and the NEC (formed by Birmingham Corporation and Chamber of Trade) are within Solihull. Yet there is no hint of this in any name, leading the visitor to believe, perhaps, that he is in Birmingham. The names of Elmdon and Bickenhill should be perpetuated, perhaps at the Airport and Station, and Solihull must earnestly resist any attempt at absorption.

The remaining fields, hedges and winding lanes ought, wherever possible, to be preserved, for the unspoiled landscape bears witness to the past and there is still much to learn about the area historically. Arden is unique and there is still a chance of discovering its remaining secrets. Detailed surveys, similar to that at Barston, should be carried out. If development has to take place then time ought to be given for investigation. Old place-names are also part of our heritage; they should be carried forward to reflect what has gone before, preferably in the place to which they refer.

Solihull is still a most pleasant place to live and it would be a sad day indeed if 'Urbs in Rure' should become 'Rure in Urbs'.

★ ★ ★ ★ ★

'All, all are vanish'd! like the fleeting Forms
Drawn in an Evening Cloud.'

115

ABOVE: The old brickworks and fields beyond, now the site of Brookes Hotel, nearing completion. (SL) BELOW: The Homeloans HQ, newly built in Homer Road. (JW)

A last glimpse of the past: the Crown Inn, Shirley, the second inn of this name on the site. Its successor has recently been demolished and replaced by Jefferson's. (DG)

Bibliography

Adams, J.C. *Hampton in Arden* (1951)

Alcock, N.W. *Warwickshire Grazier and London Skinner, 1532-1555* (Records of Social and Economic History) (1981)

Belton, J.J. *The Story of Nuthurst-cum-Hockley Heath* (1948)

—, *The Story of Packwood* (1951)

Bickley, W.B. (transcribed) *The Register of the Guild of Knowle 1451-1535* (1894)

Bishop, G.L. (transcribed) *Solihull Parish Book, 1525-1720*, 2 vols (1977)

Booth, D.T.N. *Warwickshire Watermills* (1978)

Burman, J. *Shirley and its Church*, (Revised Edition) (1968)

—, *Solihull and its School* (1949)

—, *The Story of Tanworth* (1930)

Burman, J. *Warwickshire People and Places* (1936)

Burnett, W. Barston Reports (unpublished papers)

Byng, Hon. J. *The Torrington Diaries* (1954)

Chambers, J.D. *Population, Economy, and Society in Pre-Industrial England* (1972)

Cleary, A.S.E. *The Ending of Roman Britain* (1989)

Clinker, C.R. *The Birmingham and Derby Junction Railway* (Dugdale Society Occasional Paper) (1956)

Clive, M. (Edited diaries) *Caroline Clive* (1949)

Cossons, A. Warwickshire Turnpikes (*Transactions of Birmingham and Warwickshire Archaeological Society*) vol 64

Downing, T.W. *The Records of Knowle* (1914)

Dugdale, W. *Antiquities of Warwickshire*, vol II (1730)

Finnemore, T.J. A Saltway across Arden (*TBWAS*) (1976/7)

Gelling, M. *Place Names in the Landscape* (1984)

—, *Signpost to the Past* (1978)

Gibbs, D.E. *Berkswell Through A Looking Glass* (1989)

Gover, Mawer & Stenton. *Place Names of Warwickshire* (1936)

Green, C.W. *Castle Bromwich in Times Past* (1984)

Hannett, J. *Forest of Arden* (1863)

Holyoak, M.C. *Around Chelmsley in Times Past* (c1983)

Hudson, M. Study of Barston 1843-1968 (unpublished thesis)

Malley, B. *Solihull and the Catholic Faith* (1939)

Miller, G. *Warwickshire*, (The Parishes of the Worcester Diocese) (1888)

Ogilby, J. *Road Maps of England and Wales 1675* (1971)

Orpen, P.K. Recruitment Patterns of the Schoolmaster in the 17th Century. *Warwickshire History* Vol IV No. 3

Pemberton, R. *Solihull and its Church* (1905)

Pevsner, N. & Wedgwood, A. *Warwickshire*, (The Buildings of England) (1966)

Powrie, J. Jordan, M. & Andrews, C. *Olton Heritage* (1986)

Rackham, O. *The History of the Countryside* (1986)

Roberts, B.K. Moated Homesteads in the Forest of Arden (*TBWAS*) (1976)

—, Settlement, Land Use and Population in the Western Forest of Arden 1086-1350, vols I-III (unpublished thesis)

Rowlands, M.B. *The West Midlands from AD 1000*, (A Regional History of England) (1987)

Sargent, C.P. *History of Christ Church Solihull* (1975)

Seaby, W.A. *Warwickshire Windmills* (1979)

Seaby, W.A. & Smith, A.C. *Windmills in Warwickshire* (1977)

Sherwood, R.E. *Civil Strife in the Midlands 1642-51* (1974)

Sibree, J. & Caston, M. *Independency in Warwickshire*

Skipp, V. *Crisis and Development* (1978)
—, *Discovering Bickenhill* (1963)
—, *Discovering Sheldon* (1960)
—, *Origins of Solihull* (1977)
—, *The Centre of England* (1979)
—, Contributory Chapter in *The Origins of Open-field Agriculture* (edited T. Rowley) (1981)
Smith, A. *Berkswell 1888-1988* (1988)
Smith, K.J. (Edited) *Warwickshire Apprentices and Their Masters 1710-1760* (1975)
Sutherland, G. *Elementary Education in the 19th Century* (1971)
Thomas, N. Archaeological Gazetter of Warwickshire (*TBWAS*) (1974)
Tucker, J. *Berkswell 1550-1660* (1983)
Upton, A.A. *The Collegiate Church of Saints John Baptist, Laurence and Anne of Knowls* (1966)
Van Wart, I. *Souvenir of Country Scenes and Field Sports* (1880)
Woodall, J. & Varley, M. *Looking Back at Solihull* (1987)
—, *Solihull Place Names* (1979)
—. *Welcome to Solihull* (1984)
Wootton, E. *The History of Knowle* (1972)

Annals of the Warwickshire Hunt 1795-1890
Berkswell Church Guide (1972)
Berkswell Miscellany Vols I-V
Birmingham and its Regional Setting (British Association for the Advancement of Science) (1950)
Birmingham University Extra-Mural Group 1960-74 (unpublished papers)

Directories
Documents, Surveys and Rolls at Warwickshire County Record Office, British Museum & Public Record Office.
History of Chelmsley Wood (Chelmsley Library)
History of Kingshurst (Denise Biddle and group)
Marriage Registers for Elmdon, Hampton, Berkswell and Meriden
Meriden Church Guide
Ordnance Survey *Geological Drift Maps*
—, *Warwickshire* 1st Edn 6" (1886)
Solihull Archaeological Group News Sheets 1-6
Solihull Draft Unitary Development Plan (1990)
Solihull Parish Registers 1538-1668 (1904)
Solihull Rate Book 1806
Solihull Town Guides
The Solihull Bowling Club (A Brief History)
The Victoria County History of Warwick, vols 1, 2, 4, 5, 7 & 8
Warwick County Records Vols I-IX
West Midlands Sites and Monuments Record
Wills and Inventories at Lichfield Joint Record Office
Worcestershire Recusant Vol 5 & 6 (1965)

Index

Figures in italics refer to illustrations

Subscribers

Presentation Copies

1 The Metropolitan Borough of Solihull
2 The Libraries & Arts Department, Solihull
3 Solihull Society of Arts
4 Warwick County Record Office
5 Cllr Ken Meeson
6 Cllr Richard Lewis

7   John & Joy Woodall
8   Clive & Carolyn Birch
9   Penny Woodall
10 Frank Shaw
11 Janet Ellen de Rosario Fialho
12 Clive Day
13 Colin A. Cornish
14 Mrs C.M. Dyhouse
15 Mrs H.L. Owen
16 City of Birmingham Museums & Art Gallery
17 Miss G.E. Hall
18 R.B. Cooper
19 Mrs W. Gough
20 Robert C. James
21 John Arnold
22 James H. Reid
23 Dr M.E. Scull
24 H.V. Gray
25 G.B. Green
26 Kingshurst Junior School
27 H. Brown
28/31 Cllr R.J. Herd
32 A. Garrett
33 Thomas J. Warner
34 Mrs Ann Harris
35 Mr Greenhowe
36 Mr Vince
37 Mrs Barbara Seaman
38 Mrs Linda Allen
39 Mrs J. Thorley
40 Mrs G.H. Bates
41 P.J. Lovett
42 Mrs Linda Dennis
43 Mr & Mrs P.H. Andrews
44 T.S. Camplin
45 Mrs E. Court
46 Councillor & Dr Balmer
47 R.A. Millington
48 C.R. Scurrell
49 Dr & Mrs B.V. Robinson
50 Mr & Mrs R.H. Simpson
51 H.D. Kettle
52 D. Hunt
53 Mrs D.L. Herbert
54 Mrs D.I. Webber
55 A.W. Evans
56 Miss A. Wheelock
57 N.P. Cleaver
58 J.S. Hannaford
59 Mrs O.N. Hadley
60 K.A. Gillies
61 H.M. Scharf
62 Miss H. Jacobs

63 Mrs G.A. Woodward
64 Mrs K. Musgrave
65 P. Martin
66 L.A. Davis
67 Joseph Jackson
68 Laura Kate Townson
69 Matthew Alan Townson
70 Mr & Mrs P.G. Moorman
71 J.C. Blundell
72 Miss J. Thorneycroft
73 Mr & Mrs M. Love
74 Miss Betty Bryant
75 Mr & Mrs J. Marks
76 John L. Ashford
77 M.E. Jones
78 Mrs J.M. Wright
79 Mrs A.E. Kettle
80 Mrs P. Matson-Smith
81 Mrs G. Tune
82 R.G. Everitt
83 Mrs S.Gee
84 D. Freeman
85 Mrs L. Cakebread
86 Mrs J. Parkin
87 Nicholas Parkin
88 Susan Robbins
89 Lynsey Stait
90 Julian Lendon FLA FRSA
91 M.G. Johnson
92 Mrs D. Thomas
93 Malcolm Peter Gee
94 R.S.L. Buckingham
95 Mrs P.R. Morton
96 Mrs Jean Barrow
97 A.G. Cave
98 Mrs A. Hands
99 Miss Merrick
100 Mrs Judith Jollie
101 D. Brinsmead
102 C.G. Cook
103 Audrey Joan Osborn
104 Frances Rumball
105 Moira Thompson
106 The Earl of Aylesford
107 C.G. Hoddinott

108 Mrs C.A.P. Williams
109 Mrs J.A. Taylor
110 Mrs J.J. Cooper
111 James Farrar
112 Stephen & Margaret Eyre
113 J.M. Waltham
114 D.A.D. Reeve
115 Mrs G.M. Sprang
116 Mr & Mrs David R. Patterson
117 W.H. Vine
118 Mrs P. Harbour
119 Mrs Monica J. Penn
120 B.B. Keyte
121 Joyce E. Griffiths
122 Mrs B. Lancaster
123 Miss K.L. Southall
124 Mrs D. Coolter
125 J.R. Robson
126 A.P. Salt
127 B. Williams
128 Mrs R. Shore
129 Mr Skitt
130 P.R. Siddall
131 Mrs H.P.A. Lovell
132 Mrs T. Powell
133 Mr Lucas
134 B.T. Shotton
135 Mrs B.J. Edwards
136 Mr Watt
137 Mrs J. Newey
138 Joan Felkin
139 Mrs M.E. Cooper
140 J.T. Waters
141 S.J. Felton
142 A.R.D. Hughes
143 A.E. Rudge
144 J.S. Heath
145/146 Mrs Cicely M. Ross
147 Mrs Joyce Hazlehurst
148 W.S. Harrington
149 Dr C.F. Hawkins
150 Mrs D.J. Jennens
151 Jeremy G. Solihull
152 W. Thorpe
153 Mrs M. Friswell

154 John Yates
155 Gwen Robinson
156 Mrs Josephine Bradley Hall
157 Mrs Madeleine Davies
158 Birmingham Public
159 Libraries
160 Mrs Betty Edwards
161 Mrs P. Blow
162 Mrs P.D. Watts
163/166 M. Henry
167/168 Miss R.L. Wiseman
169 Sybil Davis
170 Richard Davis
171 Celia Cox
172 Melvyn Edward Perkins
173 City of Birmingham Museums & Art Gallery
174 Mrs Celia Rickers
175 S.C. Taylor
176 N.W. Hird
177 Susan Bates
178 Mrs Helen Tyrrell
179 Christine Adderley
180 Mrs L. Newman
181 Gordon Bragg
182 Miss Barbara Jones
183 Thomas Bragg
184 R.J. Milne
185 Gordon Mustoe
186 Councillor G. Gibbons
187 Councillor K. Samuels
188 Cllr Mrs D. Holl-Allen
189 Cllr J. Windmill
190 Gordon Mustoe
191 Janet & Michael Pepper
192 Mr & Mrs Brown
193 M.G. Drake
194 Roy Brown
195 Richard Lewis, Mayor of Solihull
196 Cllr K.I. Meeson
197 D.H. Richards
198 G.S. Bolland
199 S.K. Adams
200 J.A. Slater
201 Mrs M. Suggitt
202 Mrs B. Robinson
203 C.G. Buckley
204 Mrs E.P. Clarke
205 Mrs C.M. Heginbotham
206 Miss Brenda E. Rolfe
207 Mrs M. Gateley
208 J. Welch
209 Mr & Mrs J. Tipton

210	Mr & Mrs R. Lilley	258	Warwick County
211	Miss Amanda Denton-		Record Office
	Hawkes	259	P. Callaghan
212	Mrs R. Obrook	260	Birmingham City
213	John M. Brand		Council
214	John Salt	261	K.J. Davies
215	Mrs J. Condon	262	Tidbury Green School
216	Solihull VIth Form	263	D.E. Winterbottom
	College Library	264	Mrs G.M. Edgington
217	Mrs J. Condon	265	J.L. Robson
218	Mrs B. Middleton	266	
219	T. Locke	267	P.O. Scott
220	Mrs D. Banks	268	Barbara & Graham
221	Greswold Primary		Johnson
	School	269	P.J.E. Mace
222	I.D. Carmell	270	Brian Gough
223	Coppice Junior School	271	Mrs. Y. Klidjian
224	Mrs M.J. Barlow	272	Tony Davies
225	Mr & Mrs M.	273	Mrs Annette Hardy
	Townson	274	Barbara Shaw
226	Mr & Mrs D.L. Noble	275	Mrs Sybil Pearce
227	Robert Addison	276	Mrs J. Pizzilli
228	Mr & Mrs W.F.	277	Dr John A. Edwards
	Laidle	278	W.G.R. Davies
229	Mrs Glass	279	Mrs Joyce Cox
230	Julia Richardson	280	F.W. Fowler
231	David Patterson	281	Mrs L. Winnett
232	Mrs A. Whittall	282	Mrs Christine Hall
233	Peter May	283	Mrs Karlene Madeline
234	A.E.H. May		Adams
235	Mrs M. Taylor	284	Mrs S. John
236	Mrs B. Grace	285	M.L. Prickett
237	Mrs C.M. Jones	286	Mrs P. Goddard
238	Kit Startin	287	Colin Tullett
239	Mrs A. Langford	288	R.J. & D.N. Thomas
240	Mrs M.M. Clarke	289	Mrs D.A. Hammond
241	John Bentley	290	R.G. Butcher
242	Clive Bentley	291	Mrs B.D. Gibbs
243	Jessie L. Tickell	292	Jonathan Neace
244	Mrs E. Pountney	293	W.V. Davis
245	Miss Betty M. Harris	294	Mrs B. Palmer
246	D.W. Green	295	G.K. & M.J. Williams
247	Gwendoline Ellen	296	Dr R.G. Cockerham
	Wright	297	Mrs A.F. Hore
248	J.K. Graham	298	Mrs E.J. Berry
249	A.C. Winspur	299	
250	J.W. Honnor	300	Mrs B. Walden
251	G.M. Brain	301	John Skidmore
252	Mrs B.M. Bancroft	302	Mr & Mrs John
253	Miss G. Hooper		Warner
254	G. McLarnon	303	Mr & Mrs Eric
255	G. Leighton Bishop		Warner
256	John L. Bishop	304	Mrs M.J. Devonshire
257	Susan M. McCauley	305	Miss M.R. Hill

306	Mrs P. Oakes	354	K.D. Govier
307	Mr & Mrs J.W.	355	Mrs Sally Thomas
	Arrowsmith	356	Mr Graham
308	Mrs D.M.F. Besford	357	Mr & Mrs W.R.B.
309	Barbara & Ron Siviter		Reed
310	Margaret & Derek	358	Westwood Library
	Meaking	359	Dr & Mrs J.G. Ayres
311	James Hiley	360	Mr & Mrs C.
312	Mrs B. Davies		Johnston
313	Mrs M. Garwood	361	Mrs K.S. Pond
314	John Clark	362	Brookes Hotel,
315	Elizabeth Smith		Solihull
316	T.R. Gomm	363	Vivian Sloan
317	Mr & Mrs L. Wood	364	F. Hogg
318	Mrs Susan Yates	365	Mrs S.A. Maskell
319	R.J. Costard	366	R. Brooke
320	Mr & Mrs E.G.J.	367	R.V. Clarke
	Negus	368	P.H. Lees
321	Miss D.E. Watts	369	Roy Caulfield
322	Mrs R. Farrell	370	
323	Solihull Archaeological	371	G.I. Thompson
324	Group	372	A.K.W. Chandler
325	Mrs Barbara Shackley	373	P.G. McLauchlan
326	Ian Ormerod	374	Mr & Mrs D. Mason
327	Brian John Powell	375	Mrs M.G. Morgan
328	Simon Powell	376	Mrs Page
329	Mr & Mrs S. Ellis	377	J.B. Davis
	Aves	378	D.A. Morcom
330	M.E. Kamphouse	379	N.G. Dimmock
331	Mrs J. Whitehead	380	Mr Greenhalgh
332	Lode Heath School	381	Mr Vince
333	Mrs Connie Fell	382	S.T. Cope
334	Mrs Sandra Morris	383	Mrs A.E. Wyatt
335	Justin Morris	384	Dr R.J. Bower
336	Mrs M.J. Palethorpe	385	Mr & Mrs David
337	Arlene M. Band		Cadney
338	J.P. Ward	386	Mrs Rhoda Jones
339	Mr & Mrs T.W. King	387	Wendy Burnett
340	P.H. Lees	388	Mrs Stephanie
341	Cllr Alan Morrison		Catherine Lane
342	Sharmans Cross	389	Clive Day
	Junior School	390	Kenneth J. Wise
343	S.C. Pitt	391	Sara I. Stevens
344	Miss M. Prince	392	Stephen Nixon
345	R.L. Rigg	393	Mrs M.C. Wright
346	H.A. Henderson	394	Trevor England
347	D.J. Ward	395	Solihull Public
348	Mrs Lilla M. Fisher	432	Libraries
349	Mr & Mrs H.L.	433	Solihull Metropolitan
	Darby	482	Borough Council
350	Mrs G. Hull	483	Unlisted
351	G.R. Parsons	488	
352	Mrs M. Hollis		
353	Mrs Sylvia Redshaw		*Remaining names unlisted*

ENDPAPERS — FRONT: Conjectural map of Greater Solihull pre-1600;
BACK: A section of Greenwood's Map of Warwickshire, 1822.